MARK HANKINS

THE
BLOODLINE
OF A
CHAMPION
THE POWER OF THE BLOOD OF JESUS

REVISED & EXPANDED

MARK HANKINS
ALEXANDRIA, LA

Unless otherwise indicated, all scripture quotations are taken from the *King James Version* of the Bible.

Scripture quotations marked AMP are taken from *The Amplified Bible* copyright © 1965 , 1987 by Zondervan Corporation.

Scripture quotations marked TLB are taken from *The Living Bible* copyright © 1971 by Tyndale House Publishers, Inc.

Scripture quotations marked TCNT are taken from *The Twentieth Century New Testament* copyright © 1902 by The Flemin H. Revell Company.

Scripture quotations marked NJKV are taken from the *New King James Version* copyright © 1982 by Thomas Nelson.

Scripture quotations marked MSG are taken from *The Message* copyright © 2002 by NavPress Publishing Group.

The Bloodline of a Champion: The Power of the Blood of Jesus
Second Edition 2009

Published by
Mark Hankins Ministries Publications
P.O. Box 12863
Alexandria, LA 71315
www.markhankins.org

Printed in the United States of America.

Table of Contents

Dedication

I dedicate this book to my parents, Pastors B.B. and Velma Hankins, who are now in Heaven with the Lord. They pastored for over 50 years and truly served their generation according to the will of God (Acts 13:36).

Endorsements

I have known Mark Hankins and his family for over 25 years. I have known him as an evangelist and a pastor. The message about having faith in the blood of Jesus that he preaches is life changing and energizing. Mark has great depth to his teaching, and a great calling and anointing upon his life. I consider him to be one of my good friends. Mark Hankins, in my opinion, is the prince of preachers. You will be tremendously blessed as you study his teaching and allow your faith to increase.

~ Jesse Duplantis

The message that Mark Hankins shares in his new book, *The Bloodline of a Champion*, is a message that will forever be vital to the Body of Christ. Now more than ever, the Church needs to have a deeper understanding of the power that is in His blood. The blood enables us to come into God's presence with confidence, and from that place of fellowship, we can affect change in our families, our cities, our nation, and around the world.

~ Mac and Lynne Hammond

Perfect redemption, thorough cleansing, access into the holiest, and victory in every conflict are all ours through the sacrificial offering of Christ's blood. Through intense study and personal revelation given by the Holy Spirit, Mark Hankins has put in print rich insights on the powerful subject of the blood of Christ. The Body of Christ will be richly strengthened and blessed as they read this book and make application of these great truths.

~ William E. Behrman

The message in *The Bloodline of a Champion* is a *must* for anyone wanting to live an overcoming life – a champion life. Over the years, songs about the power of the blood of Jesus, its preciousness, and its saving and redeeming qualities have been gloriously sung by the Church. Why is the power of Jesus' blood something to sing about? What makes it so precious? How does it help us in prayer? What did the blood of Jesus actually accomplish and does it still have a working function today? This dynamic message on the blood of Jesus serves as a floodlight in answering these questions and more. Be filled with courage from this straightforward instruction. Rise up and use the blood to overcome and be a champion in this life!

~ Patsy Cameneti

THE BLOOD
POWER TO ENTER
THE HOLIEST

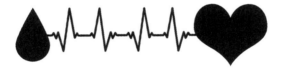

HAVING THEREFORE, BRETHREN, BOLDNESS TO
ENTER INTO THE HOLIEST BY
THE BLOOD OF JESUS.
~ HEBREWS 10:19

Introduction

While shopping for a new cell phone, I purchased a special model my son had recommended. All I needed was an instrument to make calls on, but this latest model had many more functions and applications than just a telephone. With the touch of a finger, I could access my contacts, e-mail, internet, GPS, weather, the newspaper, camera, and photo album. All I needed was a phone, but this instrument could be a dictionary, Bible, or even a directory to my favorite coffee shop! All I needed to do was explore the applications.

Sometimes Christians think they know all about the blood of Jesus, but there is much more to learn. Yes, it washes away our sin and prepares us for Heaven; still the Holy Spirit is urging the Church to increase in knowledge and application of the powerful blood of Jesus. By it we will overcome in these last days.

As you read and study this book, allow the Holy Spirit to teach you all the many applications God has provided in the blood of Jesus.

CHAPTER 1

The Bloodline of a Champion

*For whatsoever is born of God overcometh the world:
and this is the victory that overcometh the world, even
our faith.*

~   *1 John 5:4*

American Pharaoh was the winner of the coveted 2015 Triple Crown title for thoroughbred racehorses. This extraordinary racehorse won the Kentucky Derby, Preakness, and Belmont Stakes — a phenomenal achievement. What grabbed my attention, however, was his heritage.   American Pharaoh is the great, great, great grandson of Secretariat, who was the winner of the Triple Crown in 1973.   Secretariat was the beloved champion thoroughbred whose records, set forty years, ago, are still unbroken to this day. What made him outstanding was not only his physique, but also his pedigree, which he passed on to the champions in his bloodline. One of those thoroughbreds, as mentioned before, was American Pharaoh. He became the twelfth horse in this bloodline to win the Triple Crown.

It was interesting to see just how many championship racehorses were actually in Secretariat's bloodline. In fact, the top five finishers in the Kentucky Derby and all the contenders in the 2015 Preakness were descendants of Secretariat. One of his grandsons, Storm Cat, was among the preeminent stallions of his time. Storm Cat's owners had sired him 1,400 times, and there were those who were willing to pay $500,000 just to breed him once! Greatness was in his blood.

> ### *You are in the Bloodline of a Champion. You are in the Bloodline of Jesus Christ!*

American Pharaoh shares the same characteristics as his famous great, great, great grandfather, Secretariat. One observer said about him: "He can run in the mud or on dry tracks, on the rail or to the outside, come from behind or stay in the lead." Generations later, the same championship status is in his bloodline.

THE CHAMPIONSHIP PEDIGREE

In the world of championship horse breeding, the pedigree of the sire defines the value and expectation set on those in his bloodline. Likewise, Christians have been "re-fathered" by God, which puts us in the bloodline of Christ, the Firstborn from the dead. Jesus' pedigree is one of complete victory in every area of life. Jesus won in three places: hell, Heaven, and the heart of the believer. He triumphed over HELL and all of the devil's works; His blood has opened Heaven and gives us boldness in the very presence of God. It reaches into the HEARTS of believers and removes the guilt and stain of sin. The blood of Jesus purges our conscious and silences the voice of self-condemnation.

Jesus Christ is the greatest champion of all time. His Name is famous. He overcame tremendous adversity, rejection, betrayal, crucifixion, and even death. If you have been born of God, you are an overcomer with His pedigree. You should never say, "I'm only human." Instead, because you share Christ's bloodline, you should say, "I'm also human." God has a reputation for taking some real losers and making them champions!

But ye are a chosen generation, a royal priesthood, an holy nation, a peculiar people; that ye should shew forth the praises of him who hath called you out of darkness into his marvelous light.

~ *1 Peter 2:9*

You are a show-stock people.

~ *Jordan*

Therefore if any man be in Christ, he is a new creature: old things are passed away; behold, all things are become new.

~ *2 Corinthians 5:17*

YOU ARE VALUABLE: PURCHASED WITH PRECIOUS BLOOD

Forasmuch as ye know that ye were not redeemed with corruptible things, as silver and gold, from your vain conversation received by tradition from your fathers; But with the precious blood of Christ, as of a lamb without blemish and without spot.

~   *1 Peter 1:18,19*

God has a reputation for taking some real losers and making them champions!

The value placed on a thoroughbred colt is high due to the price paid to breed him in a championship bloodline. We are valuable because of the high price Jesus paid to redeem us. Jesus' precious blood was the payment to bring us into CHAMPIONSHIP STATUS. We are a new breed, born to win in His Name (2 Corinthians 5:17).

"And from Jesus Christ, who is the faithful witness, and the first begotten of the dead, and the prince of the kings of the earth. Unto him that loved us, and washed us from our sins in his own blood, And hath made us kings and priests unto God and his Father; to him be glory and dominion forever and ever. Amen," Revelations 1:5-6. In Jesus' bloodline, we have the power to overcome sin (1 John 3:9). Sin's dominion has been broken. We are loved, blood washed, and made kings and priests unto God. We are always triumphant in Christ Jesus (2 Corinthians 2:14).

EXERCISE FAITH IN THE BLOOD OF JESUS

More knowledge concerning the blood of Jesus will increase our faith (Romans 3:25 and Romans 10:17). Faith in His blood explodes when we know what it has done for us, what it purchased for us, and what it will do in us.

"Faith is largely dependent on knowledge. If knowledge of what the blood can accomplish is not accurate, then faith expects little, and the more powerful effects of the blood are limited. Feeble

6

ideas of its power prevent the deeper and more perfect manifestations of its effects."

~ **Andrew Murray**

Through increased faith in the blood of Jesus, the Church will rise to defeat the powers of darkness. This is the victory that overcomes the world. Remember this: what was true about the great Secretariat and his descendants is true about every person who has been born of God: "You can run in the mud or on dry tracks, on the rail or to the outside, come from behind or stay in the lead." *You are in the Bloodline of the Champion. You are in the Bloodline of Jesus Christ!*

Jesus' blood alone is the only thing that can cleanse us from sin nature and the condemnation

it brings.

CHAPTER 2

Faith in His Blood

Being justified freely by his grace through the redemption that is in Christ Jesus: Whom God hath set forth to be a propitiation through faith in his blood, to declare his righteousness for the remission of sins that are past, through the forbearance of God; To declare, I say, at this time his righteousness: that he might be just, and the justifier of him which believeth in Jesus. Where is boasting then? It is excluded. By what law? of works? Nay: but by the law of faith.

~ *Romans 3:24-27*

As believers, it is our duty to have faith in the blood of Jesus. Our righteousness without Him is as filthy rags and there is nothing that can be done through our own endeavors to earn peace with God. His blood alone is the only thing that can cleanse us from the sin nature and the condemnation it brings. "Not by works of righteousness which we have done, but according to his mercy he saved us, by the washing of regeneration, and renewing of the Holy Ghost," Titus 3:5. There is cleansing, washing power in Jesus' blood. It can even wash your genes!

OVERCOMING THE EBOLA VIRUS

In 2015 in Liberia, there was a deadly outbreak of the Ebola disease. Reports and pictures of the effects of Ebola dominated the news, especially when it was discovered that an American missionary, Dr. Kent Brantley, fell ill to this dreaded virus. There was no known cure for Ebola at the time, and Brantley discovered his own outbreak after having cared for Liberians with Ebola.

An experimental drug, in extremely limited supply, called ZMapp was being developed, but it was a six month process. During the testing of this medicine, mice were exposed to fragments of the Ebola virus. Upon exposure, the antibodies generated within the mice's blood were harvested to created the medicine. ZMapp worked by preventing the virus from entering and infecting new cells.

An antibody is a protein, made by the body, that latches onto foreign bacteria and viruses to make them ineffective. Each antibody is designed to target and to bind a particular opponent. Effector B cells (which produce the antibodies) then clear the infection. Once cleared, these cells persist as memory cells that can survive for years or even a lifetime. In the case of ZMapp, three antibodies worked together to bind the Ebola virus.

With much prayer from his family, as well as from believers around the world, Dr. Brantley took this new treatment. After several grueling weeks of treatment, Brantley recovered and has since returned to Liberia with his family. However, before returning to Liberia, Dr. Brantley helped to save the life of an NBC cameraman, Ashoka Mukpo, who was also diagnosed with Ebola. Without hesitation, Dr. Brantley donated his once infected and now cured plasma, which was then used to save Mukpo's life. Because of Dr. Brantley's intervention, the Ebola virus was completely bound and Mukpo fully recovered. The power to overcome the deadly Ebola disease was in the blood of one man, who freely gave his blood plasma to save another.

> ***The Blood of Jesus carries all that Jesus is and all that He has done for us.***

THE OVERCOMING AND CLEANSING POWER OF JESUS' BLOOD

Because of the intervening act of love and generosity of Jesus Christ on the cross, anyone who will put faith in His precious blood will receive the power to live an overcoming life. Life is in His blood. The spotless, pure blood of Jesus is our Divine "antibody" that continues to bind the effect of sin and set anyone who receives its power completely free.

Neither by the blood of goats and calves, but by his own blood he entered in once into the holy place, having obtained eternal redemption for us. For if the blood of bulls and of goats, and the ashes of an heifer sprinkling the unclean, sanctifieth to the purifying of the flesh: How much more shall the blood of Christ, who through the eternal Spirit offered himself without spot to God, purge your conscience from dead works to serve the living God?

~ *Hebrews 9:12-14*

When sin, sickness, addiction, fear, darkness, and disease come against you, just remember that as a Christian washed in the blood, you have a blessed "antibody" working on your behalf through the redemptive work of Christ Jesus. When He became sin, He took in Himself the "disease" Adam released to mankind through his disobedience. When Jesus was raised from the dead, He stepped out of the tomb as absolute master of death in all its phases; hell and all of its hosts, satan and all his works, sin and all of its consequences. He was the first of a redeemed, restored, victorious humanity that would follow. Jesus is the Firstborn from the dead; the first Man to enter death and master it. Jesus is Lord!

Jesus, the spotless Lamb of God, carried His blood

through every temptation and test and came through victorious. In the garden of Gethsemane, Jesus sanctified Himself praying, "Not my will, but Thine be done." There is sanctifying power in His blood. When we apply it to any rebellion, disobedience, selfishness, or pride in our lives, there is power to overcome. You can even plead the blood of Jesus over your feelings.

The blood of Jesus carries all that Jesus is and all that He has done for us. The blood of Jesus and the Holy Spirit are inseparable. Where the blood of Jesus is applied, in faith, the Holy Spirit makes real within us everything Jesus has done.

Now the God of peace, that brought again from the dead our Lord Jesus, that great shepherd of the sheep, through the blood of the everlasting covenant, Make you perfect in every good work to do his will, working in you that which is well pleasing in his sight, through Jesus Christ; to whom be glory for ever and ever. Amen.

~ Hebrews 13:20-21

Strengthen (complete, perfect) and make you what you ought to be and equip you with everything good that you may carry out His will; [while He Himself] works in you and accomplishes that which is pleasing in His sight, through Jesus Christ (the Messiah)...

~ *Hebrews 13:21, Amplified*

CONFESSIONS OF FAITH

- I have been justified with God through faith in the blood of Jesus. My sin has been remitted. I have been made righteous through faith in Jesus' blood.

- Not by works of righteousness which we have done, but according to his mercy he saved us, by the washing of regeneration, and renewing of the Holy Ghost (Titus 3:5).

- Jesus has the divine antibody in His blood that has overcome sin and all the curse that sin brings. In the name of Jesus, I overcome by the blood of the Lamb and the Word of my testimony (Revelation 12:11).

- I plead and apply the blood of Jesus to my mind, my feelings, emotions and my will.

- I receive the sanctifying power of the blood of Jesus. God is making me perfect in every good work to do his will, working in me that which is well pleasing in his sight, through Jesus Christ; to whom be glory for ever and ever. Amen (Hebrews 13:20-21).

*The Blood of Jesus
is liquid love that
flows from the
very heart of God.
It is the greatest
expression of the
Father's eternal love
for humanity.*

CHAPTER 3

The Blood of Jesus: God's Liquid Love

There was a little girl in our church who was diagnosed with a rare form of lymphoma cancer. After multiple treatments, the doctors concluded that without a bone marrow transplant she would not live. If a compatible donor could be found, the infused cells of the donor would travel to the bone marrow and initiate new and healthy blood cell production.

An extensive search for the perfect match began in her family, friends, community, and even across the United States, but it seemed this donor would never be found. After several months of searching, a possible match was located. What joy there was when tests confirmed they could proceed with the bone marrow transplant of the healthy donor to this little girl, Jira!

The process involved killing off Jira's own blood cells prior to introducing the bone marrow into her body. The infused blood cells of the donor would travel to the bone marrow and then initiate blood cell production.

Results of this transplant are quite amazing and can be compared to the new birth of someone who receives Jesus as their Savior. Jira's body was drastically changed forever. Not only was the unseen bone marrow and blood type completely changed and her health restored, but Jira's skin, hair, and eye color were also forever altered to match that of the one who donated their blood. Now, if Jira ever needed an organ transplant in the future, the match would not be found in her natural family, but in that of the donor's.

> **The blood of Jesus is liquid love that flows from the very heart of God.**

Little Jira was dying from an incurable condition in her bone marrow (the source of her blood). The bone marrow transplant brought new life to Jira and changed her very nature and physical characteristics. In the same way, because of Adam's disobedience, the spiritual nature of all mankind was diseased with sin. God searched through Heaven and found Jesus Christ, the perfect match, the perfect sacrifice. Now when the sinner receives Jesus into their heart, they receives the very life from God. This life is in Jesus' blood and not only causes you to live eternally, but imparts the personality, nature, and ability of the family of God. You look different, talk different, and act different — you are a new creation In Christ!

Why would the God of the universe, Creator of Heaven and earth, concern Himself with every individual on the earth? What lengths did He go to in order to embrace us as His family? The answer found in Ephesians 2:4: "Because of and in order to satisfy the great and intense love with which He loved us…" It is what moved Him to pour out His blood. It was to satisfy His great love for the world.

> *But God commendeth his love toward us, in that, while we were yet sinners, Christ died for us.*
>
> ~ **Romans 5:8**

> *But God puts His love for us beyond all doubt by the fact that Christ died on our behalf while we were still sinners.*
>
> ~ **Romans 5:8 (TCNT)**

The blood of Jesus is liquid love that flows from the very heart of God. It is the greatest expression of the Father's eternal love for humanity. While we remained in the filthy, ugly state of sin, that precious blood was poured out on the cross. Redeeming us from the chains of sin and restoring us to right standing with God, it was the most costly sacrifice in history.

While reaching into Heaven's holiest place, the blood extends to man's lowest place. It frees mankind from Satan's dominion and carries righteousness, mercy, redemption, and healing. The blood is alive and proves God's relentless love for us.

Through faith in the blood of Jesus, we can live in the reality of our redemption. Because the blood liberates us from the curse of sin, depression, sickness, and poverty, it provides real solutions to real problems for real people. By believing and speaking, we can apply the blood to every area of our lives and become part of a new bloodline – the bloodline of a champion.

Fellowship and Dominion

The liquid love of God also brings us back into fellowship with Him and restores our dominion. In the beginning when Adam sinned, the first thing he lost was his fellowship with God.

> *And they heard the sound of the Lord God walking in the garden in the cool of the day, and Adam and his wife hid themselves from the presence of the Lord God among the trees of the garden.*
>
> ~ *Genesis 3:8 (AMP)*

Adam hid from the presence of the Lord because he no longer had right standing with God. His fellowship was broken, and he lost his dominion in the earth.

The blood of Jesus opens Heaven and opens your heart to fellowship with God.

I am so glad God had a plan to redeem us. God loved us so much that He sent Jesus, the second Adam, to bring us back into fellowship with Him. First John 1:3 says, "... truly our fellowship is with the Father and with His Son Jesus." After God restored our fellowship, He gave us back the dominion that Adam once had.

...They which receive abundance of grace and of the gift of righteousness shall reign in life by one, Jesus Christ.

~ **Romans 5:17**

Healing and Wholeness

Nothing opens your heart to receive Heaven's blessings more than fellowshipping with God. The first creation, Adam, walked in perfect health, spirit, soul, and body. When he sinned, the curse of separation from God entered humanity, bringing sickness and hatred. Jesus, the second Adam, destroyed that curse and brought complete wholeness to mankind. First Peter 2:24 says, "...by whose stripes ye were healed." By the flowing of His blood, we are healed and made whole.

Surely he hath borne our griefs, and carried our sorrows: yet we did esteem him stricken, smitten of God, and afflicted. But he was wounded for our transgressions, he was bruised for our iniquities: the chastisement of our peace was upon him; and with his stripes we are healed.

~ *Isaiah 53:4,5*

Applying the Blood

When you plead the blood of Jesus, you are applying healing to your body. The blows He suffered bring healing to you. If you are suffering mentally or emotionally, there is peace and well-being available because Jesus bore the crown of thorns and His blood was shed. His heart was broken for all who experience heartbreak in this life. He was bruised for your iniquities and guilt. A bruise is a wound underneath the surface of the skin. Negative events or circumstances can be like a bruise which affects one's entire personality, character, and lifestyle. These wounds result in addictive and damaging behaviors and thought patterns. Other methods of relief merely cover the symptoms. Only the blood of Jesus can reach into the worst blows dealt to you in life and bring such healing that even your memory is freed from the thought of them.

> *What Jesus did for us through His blood was the greatest demonstration of love there has ever been.*

When the blood of Jesus is applied in faith, you are exercising dominion over the thief who comes to steal your innocence and possessions, kill your hope, and destroy your life—here on earth and for eternity. You must apply the blood by regularly declaring your faith in it and speaking the healing scriptures found throughout the Bible. Every word of the covenant is sealed in blood. Take time to come before the presence of the Father, draw near in worship, and allow the Holy Spirit to wash you clean.

...Though your sins be as scarlet, they shall be as white as snow...

~ *Isaiah 1:18*

As you speak the Word, the blood is applied to your situation. The power of God is in His Word and His blood. When you speak in faith, the Holy Spirit will do the supernatural work of healing your mind, will, emotions, and body. Sing and worship, praise and rejoice about it. As you do, your faith will reach out and take hold of the power of God like the woman who touched the hem of Jesus' garment (Mark 5:25-34). She was completely and continuously made whole.

Christ hath redeemed us from the curse of the law, being made a curse for us: for it is written, Cursed is every one that hangeth on a tree: That the blessing of Abraham might come on the Gentiles through Jesus Christ; that we might receive the promise of the Spirit through faith.

~   *Galatians 3:13,14*

In Genesis 15, God revealed Himself to Abraham as a God of blessing, a shield, and reward. God had promised Abraham that he would be the father of a great nation, but it didn't seem possible because Abraham had no children. In verse 8 Abraham asked, "Lord God, whereby shall I know that I shall inherit it?" In other words, Abraham needed a sign that God was going to perform what He had promised. God instructed him to take the animals, split them in two, and sacrifice them. As Abraham stood in the midst of the animals and their blood, the glory of God came down, and God met with Abraham. God cut covenant with Abraham and promised to bless him and his seed. During this visitation, Abraham was given the assurance that God was going to bring the promise to pass.

Jesus was the Seed of Abraham (Galatians 3:16). When you believe and receive Jesus as Lord, you are redeemed from the curse of sin and the law. The curse of the law came upon all those who broke the law. It is explained in Deuteronomy 28. The curse of the law includes every kind of sickness, poverty, family problem and calamity.

When you become a new creation, immediately you share in the same blessing pronounced on Abraham.

Now exercise your dominion and claim the blessing that belongs to you in your bloodline! Take authority over the enemy, look him in the eye, and put Satan, fear, sickness, depression, and poverty under your feet! Resist the devil, and he will flee from you. God will back you up, and you will experience complete freedom and joy. That's the Gospel!

What Jesus did for us through His blood was the greatest demonstration of love there has ever been. Now the flowing of the blood of Jesus is a continual reminder of His great love for us. As we exercise faith in the blood of Jesus, He brings life, healing, victory, blessing, and restoration to us.

> *Nay, in all these things we are more than conquerors through him that loved us.*
>
> ~ *Romans 8:37*

> *Listen! In all things Jesus our great Leader has established us as invincible champions through His amazing provision for us.*
>
> ~ *Romans 8:37 (Richert)*

Confession of Faith

- God proved He loved me by Jesus dying for me while I was still a sinner (Romans 5:8).

- Because of the abundance of grace and gift of righteousness, I reign in life by the blood (Romans 5:17).

- Jesus bore my griefs, carried my sorrows, transgressions, iniquities, and punishment for my peace. By His stripes, I am healed (Isaiah 53:4,5).

- Christ became a curse for me on the cross so that I could be free (Galatians 3:13).

- Christ has redeemed me from the curse of the law. I am redeemed from sin and sickness and have received the promise of the Spirit through faith. I boldly confess that through the blood of Jesus, I am healed in my mind, my will, my emotions, and my body. I am blessed with Abraham's blessing of spiritual life, prosperity, and health because of the blood of Jesus (Galatians 3:14). I thank God for the blood of Jesus!

The blood that availed so powerfully in heaven and over hell is all-powerful in a sinner's heart, too. It is impossible for us to think too highly of, or to expect too much from, the power of Jesus' blood.

~ Andrew Murray

CHAPTER 4

Divine DNA

Some of the finest horses in the world are bred and sold in Lexington, Kentucky. Worth millions of dollars, these horses live on the finest farms and the most beautiful ranches. Sometimes, these thoroughbreds even live better than most people!

When visiting Lexington, we flew into the same airport where the prince of Saudi Arabia has his 747 private jet. He owns one of the nicest ranches there and has some of these 50 million dollar horses. While I was there, I asked about these thoroughbreds. Just as I said before, the breeding fee on this one particular horse that had a champion producing bloodline was $500,000. In other words, that is what you would pay if you wanted to have a colt that came from that horse. These horses are so expensive because they have the bloodline of a champion, like that of American Pharoah who came from Secretariat. I thought, *Is it worth $500,000 for the chance to produce a champion?*

Divine DNA

Breeders carefully protect the lineage of fine animals and know the history reaching far into their ancestry. Records are kept, prizes and trophies are displayed, and famous names are spoken of from generation to generation. Let's look at the meaning of bloodline, lineage, and progenitor.

> *Bloodline* – *a sequence of direct ancestors especially in a pedigree*
>
> *Lineage* – *race; progeny; descendants in a line from a common progenitor*
>
> *Progenitor* – *a biologically related ancestor; a progenitor of species. A person or thing that indicates a direction, originates something, or serves as a model; predecessor*

> *Jesus is the Champion Son of God and Son of Man. He has a history of producing champions.*

The greater the victory, the greater the value the progenitor has. Royalty is bred into a champion and is passed from generation to generation.

In Christ, God established a bloodline of champions. There are winning traits in this bloodline. First Peter 2:9 says, "We are a chosen generation, a royal priesthood, an holy nation, a peculiar people...." Jesus is the Champion Son of God and Son of Man. His assignment was to bring many sons into glory. He has a history of producing champions. When you study His bloodline of faith, you find men and women who have changed the world. When you were born again, you were born of that divine seed. You are an heir of God and joint heir with Jesus! You have some genetics in you now that make you a thoroughbred!

Being born again, not of corruptible seed, but of incorruptible, by the word of God, which liveth and abideth for ever.

~ 1 Peter 1:23

God wants you to know what is on the inside of you. When you were born again, you were not born of the will of the flesh nor of the will of man—you were born of God! You were re-fathered by God! Through Jesus Christ, God established the bloodline of a champion. The same life that is in Him is in you!

> *The blood of Jesus still carries the right ingredients to produce champions today.*

Never Underestimate Genetics

Thoroughbreds just flat know who they are. They walk differently. They do not walk like mules because they know who they are. Do you remember the movie *Seabiscuit*? It is the story of a racehorse who was racing for the championship. His manager said, "Just let that big fancy horse get right up next to him and look him in the eye—that's all it will take!" Seabiscuit took the challenge and won the race.

Sometimes all it takes to win is circumstances looking you right in the eye. Something kicks in on the inside of you because there is a champion that has been born in you.

It is bred in you — it's in your blood! The blood of Jesus still carries the right ingredients to produce champions today. Through faith in His blood, we are changed.

You Belong in the Winner's Circle

For whatsoever is born of God overcometh the world: and this is the victory that overcometh the world, even our faith.

> ~   *1 John 5:4*

Whatsoever is born of God overcomes the world. This is the victory that overcomes the world — even our faith. Even though God has produced this bloodline in you through Christ, it is still not automatic. You still have to believe. The biggest fight of your life will be the faith fight. When doubt and fear come, and you are surrounded by circumstances that make you want to quit, you have to go back to the Word of God and hold fast to your profession of faith. You have to say, "I am who God says I am. I can do what God says I can do. Jesus Christ is in me and He is the Champion!"

You have been born of God. God is your Father, Jesus is your older brother, and the same Spirit of life that raised

Christ from the dead is on the inside of you! You are washed in the blood of Jesus!

The Blood of Jesus Is Supernatural

And hath made of one blood all nations of men for to dwell on all the face of the earth...

~ *Acts 17:26*

Man's blood was contaminated when Adam sinned. This condition was passed on to the whole human race. Ezekiel 16:6 says, "And when I passed by thee, and saw thee polluted in thine own blood, I said unto thee when thou wast in thy blood, Live...."

Adam was a type or pre-figure of Him that was to come (Romans 5:14). In Jesus Christ, the last Adam, God established a new bloodline. The blood of Jesus carries the life of the new creation. Second Corinthians 5:17 says, "Therefore if any man be in Christ, he is a new creature: old things are passed away; behold, all things are become new."

Jesus has redeemed us to God by His blood. The blood of Jesus is not natural human blood. He was born of a virgin and conceived by the Spirit of God. His blood is supernatural — in origin and in power. The blood not only has power in the earth today, but is also eternally honored in Heaven.

> *And they sung a new song, saying, Thou art worthy to take the book, and to open the seals thereof: for thou wast slain, and hast redeemed us to God by thy blood out of every kindred, and tongue, and people, and nation; And hast made us unto our God kings and priests: and we shall reign on the earth. And I beheld, and I heard the voice of many angels round about the throne and the beasts and the elders: and the number of them was ten thousand times ten thousand, and thousands of thousands; Saying with a loud voice, Worthy is the Lamb that was slain to receive power, and riches, and wisdom, and strength, and honor, and glory, and blessing. And every creature which is in heaven, and on the earth, and under the earth, and such as are in the sea, and all that are in them, heard I saying, Blessing, and honor, and glory, and power, be unto him that sitteth upon the throne, and unto the Lamb forever and ever. And the four beasts said, Amen. And the four and twenty elders fell down and worshiped him that liveth forever and ever.*
>
> ~   *Revelation 5:9-14*

In this book, we will be studying the power of the blood of Jesus. Not only will we discuss what it has done *for us* but also what it will do *in us*. We will also see the importance of applying the blood in order to be effective in our lives. Because of His blood, all believers are included in the genealogy of Jesus Christ. By faith we are a part of a new bloodline — the bloodline of a champion.

Confession of Faith

- I have been born again, not of the will of man, but of God (1 Peter 1:23).

- I have been born of God so I overcome the world. The victory that overcomes the world is my faith (1 John 5:4).

- I am in Christ. I am a new creature; old things are passed away and all things have become new (2 Corinthians 5:17).

- I am a king and priest to God, and I shall reign with Christ by His blood (Revelation 5:9,10).

He who once gave His blood for us will surely, every moment, impart its effectiveness. Trust Him to do this. Trust Him to open your eyes and to give you a deeper spiritual insight. Trust Him to teach you to think about the blood as God thinks about it. Trust Him to impart to you, and to make effective in you, all that He enables you to see.

~ Andrew Murray

CHAPTER 5

God's Meeting Place

What is the glory of God? The glory of God is His manifested presence, His goodness, His mercy, and His compassion. It includes all of the advantages, favor, blessing, wealth, and provision of God. The Bible is the story of how God restores His glory to man. God reverses what Satan did in Adam and brings restoration through the blood of Jesus Christ.

[All] are justified and made upright and in right standing with God, freely and gratuitously by His grace (His unmerited favor and mercy), through the redemption which is [provided] in Christ Jesus, Whom God put forward [before the eyes of all] as a mercy seat

and propitiation by His blood the cleansing and life-giving sacrifice of atonement and reconciliation, [to be received] through faith...

~ *Romans 3:24,25 (AMP)*

Jesus took the sin of the past and He paid that debt. Then He reached into the future and He paid for the sin of the future. How do we receive that victory or that forgiveness? We receive victory and forgiveness through faith in His blood.

The Bible tells us we have *propitiation* through the blood of Jesus. The word *propitiation* means "reconciliation" or "restoration to fellowship, friendship, or favor." In other words, we have been restored to fellowship and favor with God by faith in the blood.

The Mercy Seat

And there I will meet with thee, and I will commune with thee from above the mercy seat, from between the two cherubim which are upon the ark of the testimony, of all things which I will give thee in commandment unto the children of Israel.

~ *Exodus 25:22*

The Amplified translation of Romans 3:25 also calls redemption through Christ the "mercy seat" or God's meeting place. In the Old Testament, the mercy seat on the Ark of the Covenant was the place where the priests applied the blood. It was also the place of God's glory and presence. At the mercy seat, God met with His people and communed with them.

Appropriately named, the mercy seat also represents God's infinite mercy. We can never do anything to deserve God's restoration to favor. Our access into the holiness of God is both initiated and finished by the mercy of God. Nothing we do can merit His forgiveness; we are saved not by works of righteousness, but by God's mercy. He is so rich in mercy! The Bible says His mercies are new every morning. He has mercy for our failures and grace for our future. He is the Father of mercies.

> *The moment you exercise faith in the blood, you will have a meeting with God.*

While the mercy seat in the Old Testament was a physical location, the New Testament mercy seat is faith in the blood of Jesus. The first benefit of faith in the blood of Jesus is that we are restored to fellowship with God. The moment you exercise faith in the blood, you will have a meeting with God.

The devil would like to take advantage of your lack of knowledge and try to destroy your life. Exercising faith in the blood of Jesus will put a stop to the devil and bring you into fellowship with God. Our faith in the blood is the means whereby God releases His blessing into our lives.

Faith in the blood of Jesus brings us to a state of atonement with the Father. Atonement simply means a place of unity with Christ—a place of agreement with God. In order to be in agreement with God, we must have faith in the blood.

> *God's method of justification is to give men His righteousness as a free gift. It is possible for Him to offer it completely by grace, since it comes through the redemptive death of Christ Jesus. God offered Jesus as a public sacrifice that His shed blood might cleanse us from our sins when we put our faith in Him. At the same time, this act vindicated His justice. The sacrifice of Jesus clearly showed why God, in His forbearance, was able to overlook the sins of men in the past.*
>
> ~ *Romans 3:24,25 (Lovett)*

But our Lord, by His sacrifice has made for us a way into the pardoning grace of God. His was truly a spiritual sacrifice. His blood, shed on the Cross, is the red seal of it. There is the true Mercy Seat, And the power of faith is such that by faith a man can unite himself with the divine Victim and in that union enter into the blessed state of at-one-ment with the Father.

~   *Romans 3:25 (Carpenter)*

Not Without the Blood

In the Old Testament, the people could not approach the presence of God without the blood. How many times have we tried to access the presence of God based on things other than the blood of Jesus? Thank God for the blood. God said He would meet us at the mercy seat — but not without the blood.

Now when these things were thus ordained, the priests went always into the first tabernacle, accomplishing the service of God. But into the second went the high priest alone once every year, not without blood, which he offered for himself, and for the errors of the people.

~   *Hebrews 9:6,7*

45

And almost all things are by the law purged with blood;
and without shedding of blood is no remission.

~ *Hebrews 9:22*

What does the word *remission* mean? Remission of sin includes forgiveness, but it is much more than that. Remission also includes the cancellation of a penalty and the removal of guilt. If you had a terminal disease such as cancer and went to the doctor, and he said that the cancer is now in remission, it would mean that it has stopped or become inactive. However, the doctor would probably want to check you regularly for the next five years to see if it shows up again.

> *Remission of sin includes forgiveness, the*
> *cancellation of a penalty and the removal*
> *of guilt.*

The blood from the sacrifices of goats and calves in the Old Testament only covered sin. The blood of Jesus in the New Testament is for the remission of sin. Do you believe that God has brought some things of your past into remission?

When the blood is applied by faith, the devil cannot stir up that mess from your past and make it active again. If you want to keep it in remission, you need to get up every morning saying, "The just shall live by faith and my faith is in the blood of Jesus. When His blood was shed, I was forgiven. I am redeemed, I am set free. The curse is broken; I am healed, I have access to God, and I have found the meeting place. I can meet with God through faith in the blood!"

> *Enter the Holy Place, and the most conspicuous thing is the golden altar of incense, which also, together with the veil, is constantly sprinkled with the blood. Ask what lies beyond the Holy Place, and you will be told that it is the Most Holy Place where God dwells. If you ask how He dwells there and how He is approached, you will be told "not without blood." The golden throne, where His glory shines, is itself sprinkled with the blood once every year when the high priest alone enters to bring in the blood and to worship God. The highest act in that worship is the sprinkling of the blood.*
>
> *~ Andrew Murray*

Blood Covenant

The Bible is a blood covenant. You have a covenant with God. God is a covenant — making God, and the word *covenant* means "the shedding of blood." God made a pretty radical commitment to us. Jesus is your blood brother. He whipped everything in hell. If anybody starts to mess with you, they will have to deal with Jesus, your big brother!

The harlot, Rahab, survived what happened at Jericho, not because she had done anything right other than recognizing the people of God. She may not have fit into anybody else's club, but she got into God's club by hanging that scarlet thread—the blood—outside of her window!

Every Real Diamond Has a Flaw

Several years ago, I went to buy Trina a diamond. The jeweler told me that every real diamond has a flaw or defect. I found it interesting, that the only stone that does not have a flaw is a cubic zirconium. The only problem with this stone is that it is worthless!

Hebrews 11, God's "hero" chapter, is full of people who had defects or flaws. Abraham, Isaac, Jacob, Noah, David, Samson, and Rahab—all of them were imperfect. I told God, "If I were You, I would have edited the Bible because I wouldn't want everybody to know what some of my kids did!"

How did all of these imperfect people get in this list? It was just by faith in His blood. They knew something about the blood covenant. Every one of them had a defect, everyone of them had a flaw, but their confidence was in the blood. They knew that they were not welcome into His presence by anything they did or did not do. God said, "Come on in. I declare you righteous."

The next time the devil tries to accuse you and remind you that you have some flaws and defects, you can say, "I may have some defects, but at least I am a diamond!" By full assurance of faith, you can draw near to God and make it through!

The Lamb of God

Forasmuch as ye know that ye were not redeemed with corruptible things, as silver and gold, from your vain conversation received by tradition from your fathers; But with the precious blood of Christ, as of a lamb without blemish and without spot.

~   1 Peter 1:18,19

And from Jesus Christ, who is the faithful witness, and the first begotten of the dead, and the prince of the kings of the earth. Unto him that loved us, and washed us from our sins in his own blood, and hath made us kings and priests unto God and his Father; to him be glory and dominion for ever and ever. Amen.

~ *Revelation 1:5,6*

And they sung a new song, saying, Thou art worthy to take the book, and to open the seals thereof: for thou wast slain, and hast redeemed us to God by the blood out of every kindred, and tongue, and people, and nation.

~ *Revelation 5:9*

Jesus is called the Lamb of God twenty-eight times in the book of Revelation. He redeemed us to God and purchased our freedom by His blood. You were not redeemed with silver and gold or corruptible things. You have been redeemed from your vain lifestyle or conversation by the blood of Jesus.

> *Where the blood of Jesus is honored, the Holy Spirit will work. The Holy Spirit goes where the blood flows.*

It is easy to live a vain lifestyle with no significance or purpose. God said that you have been redeemed from a life that has no meaning or significance. You have been redeemed by the blood of Jesus. You have been redeemed by the precious blood of the Lamb.

We Have an Adversary

You have an adversary, the devil, who comes to steal, to kill, and to destroy the things that God said belong to you. The devil seeks to gain access into your life, your thoughts, your family, and your finances. Peter said to be "sober" which means to be continuously wide awake and diligent.

Be sober, be vigilant; because your adversary the devil, as a roaring lion, walketh about, seeking whom he may devour.

~ *1 Peter 5:8*

The word "adversary" in 1 Peter 5:8 is the Greek word *antidikos* which means "a lawyer who is a prosecutor." What does a prosecutor do? He brings constant accusation using facts of past sins and mistakes. In other words, Satan is a prosecutor. He reminds us of our failures and tells us we deserve to be in the mess we are in. He wants us to feel unworthy and deserving of punishment and failure. The devil even knows enough scripture to leave us condemned.

> *And they overcame him by the blood of the Lamb, and by the word of their testimony; and they loved not their lives unto the death.*
>
> ~ *Revelation 12:11*

In order to overcome the devil, you have to know something about the blood of Jesus. Jesus said, "...I am come that they might have life, and that they might have it more abundantly" (John 10:10). Exercise your faith in the blood of Jesus because you know what Jesus has done for you.

Honor the Blood

> *How much more shall the blood of Christ, who through the eternal Spirit offered himself without spot to God, purge your conscience from dead works to serve the living God?*
>
> ~ *Hebrews 9:14*

Notice that the blood and the Holy Spirit work together. Where the blood of Jesus is honored, the Holy

Spirit will work. The Holy Spirit goes where the blood flows. Smith Wigglesworth said, "The moment a man is cleansed, the Holy Spirit will fall." When the blood is applied, the atmosphere of your life will change because the Holy Spirit gets involved.

> *The blood and the Spirit always bear testimony together. Where the blood is honored in faith or preaching, there the Spirit works; and where He works, He always leads souls to the blood. The Holy Spirit could not be given until the blood was shed. The living bond between the Spirit and the blood cannot be broken.*
>
> ~ *Andrew Murray*

Smith Wigglesworth said, "The Holy Spirit never brings condemnation. He always reveals the blood of Christ. He is the lifting power of the church." If you understand the power of the blood of Jesus, you can win your case because you have an advocate who is Jesus Christ. He is righteous and His blood will cleanse you from all sin. Andrew Murray said, "Let us honor the blood greatly by confessing before God that it cleanses us."

Cleansed by the Blood

Let us draw near with a true heart in full assurance of faith, having our hearts sprinkled from an evil conscience, and our bodies washed with pure water.

~ *Hebrews 10:22*

This verse says that the blood of Jesus will cleanse your heart from an evil or guilty conscience. This scripture is not referring to your physical heart. Your heart is the part of you that believes God. So if the devil can contaminate your heart, the blood of Jesus can cleanse your heart. Smith Wigglesworth said, "There is not one thing in me the blood does not cleanse."

> *The Holy Spirit never brings condemnation. He always reveals the blood of Christ. He is the lifting power of the church.*
>
> ~ *Smith Wigglesworth*

The blood of Jesus will not only cleanse your heart but also wash your body. We live in a world that is dirty. You can get dirty pretty easily because the devil is constantly suggesting thoughts against your mind, trying to bring you to a place of disobedience and sin so that he can destroy your life. But if you understand the power of the blood of Jesus, you can overcome him.

In that day there shall be a fountain opened to the house of David and to the inhabitants of Jerusalem for sin and for uncleanness.

~ *Zechariah 13:1*

The blood can reach into the secret recesses of your motives and purposes, and cleanse you from all unrighteousness, all iniquity, all sin, all shame, and all guilt. The voice of your conscience declares and agrees with the Bible that you are entirely righteous. Christ has produced a righteousness that enables you to stand before God and call Him, "Daddy," just as if you had never sinned. God looks upon me like I never did anything wrong because of the blood of His cross. The precious blood of Jesus speaks of mercy, righteousness, and perfect reconciliation. You can come boldly to the throne of grace. You can have perfect peace.

Faith Is an Act

So also faith, if it does not have works (deeds and actions of obedience to back it up), by itself is destitute of power (inoperative, dead).

~ *James 2:17 (AMP)*

Faith cannot be passive because faith without works is dead. Faith is an act. Faith acts like the Bible is true. The blood must be applied by faith. According to your faith so be it unto you.

Faith involves believing and speaking. So if you take what you know about the blood and speak it (mix faith with it, act on it, praise God with it), not only will it break the power of sin and Satan, but it will also do something inside of you. Andrew Murray once said, "Let us honor the blood greatly by confessing before God that it cleanses us."

Faith begins where the will of God is known. Once we know what the Bible says, then faith begins. We need to live by faith and continually apply the blood. There is power in the blood. We act in faith because the blood of Jesus has purchased our redemption.

Confession of Faith

- I commune with God at the mercy seat, where the blood of Jesus has been applied (Exodus 25:22).

- Through the blood I have atonement and union with the Father (Romans 3:25).

- My sin and its effects are in remission because of the shed blood of Jesus (Hebrews 9:22).

- I have been redeemed, not with corruptible things, but with the precious blood of Christ (1 Peter 1:18,19).

- I overcome the accuser by the blood of the Lamb and the word of my testimony (Revelation 12:11).

- Through the blood of the eternal Spirit, the blood purges my conscience from sin (Hebrews 9:14).

- I draw near to God with faith, the blood sprinkles my conscience, and my body is washed with pure water (Hebrews 10:22).

- The just shall live by faith, and my faith is in the blood of Jesus. Because of the blood of Jesus, I am forgiven, I am redeemed, I am set free, and I am healed.

Faith in His blood is the power and the vehicle that launches the believer into the very presence of God.

~ *Mark Hankins*

For the enjoyment of this blessedness, nothing is necessary except faith in the blood. The blood alone has done everything.

~ *Andrew Murray*

Reconciled by the Blood

Being justified freely by his grace through the redemption that is in Christ Jesus: Whom God hath set forth to be a propitiation through faith in his blood, to declare his righteousness for the remission of sins that are past, through the forbearance of God; To declare, I say, at this time his righteousness: that he might be just, and the justifier of him which believeth in Jesus...by the law of faith.

~ *Romans 3:24-27*

What a wonderful sight it is to see a space shuttle launch. You can see it rise slowly, then rocket into another world. The power, the sound, and the sight are fascinating.

The giant fuel cells that propel it are necessary to get it out of this atmosphere into outer space. The shuttle leaves the law of gravity behind and enters a world of weightlessness.

I like to compare that to faith in the blood of Jesus. Faith in His blood is the power and the vehicle that launches the believer into the very presence of God. We are launched into another realm where the new law of faith rules.

Threat Environment Removed

And, having made peace through the blood of his cross, by him to reconcile all things unto himself; by him, I say, whether they be things in earth, or things in heaven. And you, that were sometime alienated and enemies in your mind by wicked works, yet now hath he reconciled in the body of his flesh through death, to present you holy and unblameable and unreproveable in his sight.

~   Colossians 1:20-22

Christ has brought you into the very presence of God, and you are standing there before him with nothing left against you – nothing left that he could even chide you for.

~   Colossians 1:22 (TLB)

I once heard someone say, "In a threat environment, all communication is corrupted." That means if you are trying to communicate with someone and they feel threatened, they really won't hear anything you say. The threat environment makes people shut down because they are constantly trying to defend themselves.

> *Now, because of the blood of Jesus, we can come boldly into the very presence of God and know that He is not holding anything against us.*

Before God could have good fellowship with us, He had to eliminate the threat environment. Now, because of the blood of Jesus, we can come boldly into the very presence of God and know that He is not holding anything against us. In fact, the number one thing Jesus did with the blood of His cross is make peace so we can come into the presence of God without a sense of sin, guilt, or inferiority.

The law of sin and death is broken by the law of the Spirit of life in Christ Jesus. The weight of sin that once held you down is broken and you are free. Think of the possibilities and the power in the blood of Jesus.

After Jesus died and shed His blood on the cross,

paying in full the price for every man's sin, He entered Heaven on our behalf and made reconciliation *for* us. God, in Christ, intervened and through Jesus' death, reconciled us in order to make us holy, faultless, and irreproachable in His presence.

> *Neither by the blood of goats and calves, but by His own blood he entered in once into the holy place, having obtained eternal redemption for us.*
>
> ~   *Hebrews 9:12*

> *...And secured a complete redemption (an everlasting release for us).*
>
> ~   *Hebrews 9:12 (AMP)*

Believing with your heart is a personal thing. When your conscience is cleansed by the blood, your heart has confidence towards God. No one else can apply the blood of Jesus to your conscience like you can.

> *How much more shall the blood of Christ, who through the eternal Spirit offered himself without spot to God, purge your conscience from dead works to serve the living God?*
>
> ~   *Hebrews 9:14*

> *We see that though the blood has been applied in Heaven FOR us, it is also necessary that the blood be applied IN us.*

When the blood of Jesus is applied by faith to our hearts, there is a work of reconciliation accomplished *in* us. Even our conscience is purified as we apply the cleansing blood. We see that though the blood has been applied in Heaven *for* us, it is also necessary that the blood be applied *in* us. The power in the blood will then be experienced in our conscience and inmost personality. Our conscience is the voice of our spirit. Our conscience then witnesses we are cleansed and every hindrance has been removed. Intimate fellowship with God is completely restored and "as He is, so are we in this world" (1 John 4:17).

A Reconciliation of the Facts

Whom God hath set forth to be a propitiation through faith in his blood, to declare his righteousness for the remission of sins that are past, through the forbearance of God.

~ *Romans 3:25*

In this scripture, Paul is saying that we have been made right with God simply by faith in the blood. He actually uses the word *propitiation* to describe this. Probably none of you have ever used that word unless you were reading the Bible. As we studied earlier the word *propitiation* is translated in other places as "reconciliation." *Reconciliation* simply means "a restoration of fellowship" and "a restoration to favor." In other words, Paul says we have propitiation or we have been reconciled. We have been restored to fellowship and favor with God by faith in His blood!

> *Reckon ye also yourselves to be dead indeed unto sin, but alive unto God through Jesus Christ our Lord.*
>
> ~ **Romans 6:11**

The word *reconcile* is an accounting term. When you reconcile your account, you don't create the facts or figures, you simply record them. Every month your personal checking account must be reconciled with your bank statement. Your feelings don't determine the facts. You may feel like you have a certain amount of money in your account, but you'd better not go by your own estimation, but by the bank's record.

Likewise, not feeling saved, forgiven, or victorious doesn't change the facts! Every day there must be a reconciling of the facts of redemption in Heaven to your personal life here on the earth by faith. Take the record in God's Word and declare the truth saying, "I have been redeemed by the blood of Jesus and that's a fact!" In so doing, you will reconcile your personal account to Heavens' account and walk in overcoming power right where you are.

> *The blood of Jesus has many different ingredients and applications which are all applied by faith.*

Faith in the Blood of Christ

He who once gave His blood for us will surely, every moment, impart its effectiveness. Trust Him to do this. Trust Him to open your eyes and to give you a deeper spiritual insight. Trust Him to teach you to think about the blood as God thinks about it. Trust Him to impart to you, and to make effective on you, all that He enables you to see.

~ Andrew Murray

When we see clearly what Jesus has done for us through His blood, we begin our ascent into the realm of God. The blood of Jesus has many different ingredients and applications which are all applied by faith. God is a faith God and faith is what pleases Him. As we study the Word of God, our faith grows. Faith opens the door to the supernatural. I like to say that faith is what cranks God's tractor!

> *So then faith cometh by hearing, and hearing by the word of God.*
>
> ~ *Romans 10:17*

Faith is built on accurate knowledge. There is no such thing as ignorant faith. When faith cometh, substance cometh and you knoweth!

> *Faith is largely dependent on knowledge. If knowledge of what the blood can accomplish is not accurate, then faith expects little, and the more powerful effects of the blood are limited. Feeble ideas of its power prevent the deeper and more perfect manifestations of its effects.*
>
> ~ *Andrew Murray*

In order to have faith, you must understand what God says about the subject or the situation. If we are to have faith in His blood, we have to know what happened when the blood of Jesus was shed, what the blood purchased for us, and what it will do in us.

> ## *We can access the presence of God through faith in His blood.*

The entrance of thy words giveth light; it giveth understanding unto the simple.

~ **Psalm 119:130**

We can access the presence of God through faith in His blood. Without accurate knowledge, our faith is limited so that even though what Christ has done is perfect, our access to it is imperfect. Faith in His blood can produce greater results in us than we've yet known.

> *As we seek to find out what the Scriptures teach about the blood, we will see that faith in the blood, even as we now understand it, can produce greater results in us than we have yet known; and in the future, a ceaseless blessing may be ours.*
>
> ~ *Andrew Murray*

Through the blood of the everlasting covenant, you will be made perfect in every good work to do His will. You will be launched into a new level of victory and blessing as you apply the blood constantly with boldness and full assurance of faith (Hebrews 10:19-23)!

> *Now the God of peace, that brought again from the dead our Lord Jesus, that great shepherd of the sheep, through the blood of the everlasting covenant, Make you perfect in every good work to do his will, working in you that which is well-pleasing in his sight, through Jesus Christ; to whom be glory for ever and ever. Amen.*
>
> ~   *Hebrews 13:20,21*

> *Believer, I urge you, let every thought about the blood awaken in you the glorious confession, "By His own blood, the Lord Jesus has sanctified me. He has taken complete possession of me for God, and I belong entirely to God."*
>
> ~   *Andrew Murray*

There is no such thing as silent faith. Faith has a voice (Mark 11:23). Faith involves believing and speaking. We must hold fast our profession of faith in the blood of Jesus. We honor the blood of Jesus as we lift our voice in faith declaring what it has done and what it is accomplishing.

When we exercise our right of access to God, it gives Him access to our lives and needs. Every Word of God has blood on it. The spoken Word of God is the voice of the blood covenant. We must confess our faith in the blood and its power. Sing songs, hymns, and spiritual songs about the blood. Apply the blood to every situation. Praise God for the blood. Lift up your voice and declare what the blood had done for you!

Confession of Faith

- I have peace with God through the blood of His cross (Colossians 1:20).

- I was an enemy of God, but now I have been reconciled to Him. I am now unblameable in His sight (Colossians 1:22).

- I reckon myself dead to sin but alive to God through Jesus Christ (Romans 6:11).

- Christ obtained eternal redemption for me (Hebrews 9:12).

- The blood of Jesus purges my conscience from dead works to serve a living God (Hebrews 9:14).

- Faith in the blood comes to me now by hearing and hearing by the Word of God (Romans 10:17).

- Through the blood I am being perfected in every good work to do God's will (Hebrews 13:21).

The blood of Jesus must be brought by the Holy Spirit into direct contact with our hearts so that our hearts become cleansed from an evil conscience. The blood removes all self-condemnation. It cleanses the conscience. Conscience then witnesses that the removal of guilt has been so perfectly completed that there is no longer the least separation between God and us. Conscience bears witness that we are well-pleasing to God; that our hearts are cleansed; that we, through the sprinkling of the blood, are in true living fellowship with God. Yes, the blood of Jesus Christ cleanses from all sin, not only from the guilt but also from the stain of sin.

~ Andrew Murray

CHAPTER 7

Ingredients in the Blood

When I went to purchase life insurance, I was required to give a blood sample in order to be approved for a large policy. They sent my blood to the lab to study it. Under powerful microscopes, they saw the ingredients that were in my blood. A few days later, I received a full-page printout with a detailed description of what was in my blood. There were things in my blood that I couldn't even pronounce!

One of my staff members who heard me talk about what was in my blood, gave me a 12-page printout of human blood components that he had found on the internet. There are over 200 blood components included in that list. When I read all of the ingredients that are in the blood I thought, *All of that is in the blood*?

All of the human blood components work together to bring life to the body. There are also many important functions of human blood including:

- Supply of oxygen to tissues
- Supply of nutrients
- Removal of waste
- Immunological functions — circulation of white cells and detection of foreign material by antibodies
- Coagulation or self-repair mechanism
- Messenger functions
- Regulation of body pH
- Regulation of core body temperature

Your physical health is not only determined by the quality of the blood but also by the circulation of the blood. The same is true for the Body of Christ. There is a supply of life, removal of waste, immunological functions, self-repair mechanisms, and messenger functions through our faith in the blood of Jesus and fellowship with the believers.

When Jesus died on the cross, He took His blood into Heaven and purchased our eternal redemption. He applied that blood to the mercy seat and the veil in the temple was torn from the top to the bottom. God was saying, "It's open house! Anybody can come in by the blood of Jesus." God took the blood of Jesus into His divine laboratory and put it under a high-powered microscope and then He said, "Let me give you a printout of everything that is in the blood of Jesus!"

A thorough investigation of the blood of Jesus reveals every necessary ingredient for full salvation.

When we look at the New Testament, we see a full printout of the ingredients in the blood of Jesus. If we know all of the ingredients in His blood, then we can have faith for His promises. If we have faith for His promises, then the devil can't cheat us out of them. You can open your Bible and say, "I have a printout of what is in the blood of Jesus!"

A thorough investigation of the blood of Jesus reveals every necessary ingredient for full salvation. There is righteousness, forgiveness, mercy, grace, redemption, sanctification, healing, victory, blessing, boldness, prosperity, and power in the blood of Jesus! Now that's something to rejoice about! You should get so full of the Holy Spirit that if you got bit by a mosquito, he would fly off singing "There's power in the blood!"

Declared Righteous

Righteousness is one of the main ingredients in the blood. In Romans 3:21, Paul says that God has produced this righteousness through what Jesus Christ did. He said that this righteousness would come to everyone who believes. Not by works that we have done or haven't done, but simply based on what Jesus has done.

> *For all have sinned, and come short of the glory of God; Being justified freely by his grace through the redemption that is in Christ Jesus: Whom God hath set forth to be a propitiation through faith in his blood, to declare his righteousness for the remission of sins that are past, through the forbearance of God.*
>
> ~ *Romans 3:23-25*

The word *justified* in Romans 3:24 means "declared righteous" or "to be made right with God." So we have been justified and declared righteous freely by His grace through the redemption that is in Christ Jesus (Romans 3:24). God sent Jesus to be a propitiation through faith in His blood to declare His righteousness for the remission of sins that are past (Romans 3:25).

Aren't you glad that the sins of your past will have no impact upon your future? Your past has no effect on you whatsoever! Romans 3:25 says, "through faith in His blood, to declare his righteousness...." God has produced a righteousness that is His standard of righteousness through the blood of Jesus.

A Chain Reaction

For the kingdom of God is not meat and drink; but righteousness, and peace, and joy in the Holy Ghost.

~ *Romans 14:17*

...It is righteousness (that state which makes a person acceptable to God) and [heart] peace and joy in the Holy Spirit.

~ *Romans 14:17 (AMP)*

> *And the work of righteousness shall be peace; and the effect of righteousness quietness and assurance for ever.*
>
> ~   *Isaiah 32:17*

Righteousness simply means "right standing with God." The first product of this righteousness is peace. Your peace is not disturbed anymore because you are right with God. The Kingdom of God is righteousness and peace — calm; quietness; settled down; not disturbed; not upset; not fretting.

Say this out loud, "I have peace in God. My peace is not disturbed anymore because I have been made right with God! " Romans 14:17 says that joy is also a product of righteousness. Righteousness, peace, and joy in the Holy Ghost — it's a chain reaction!

Sin Consciousness Destroys Faith

Another definition of *righteousness* is "the ability to stand before God without a sense of sin, guilt, or inferiority." In other words, there is no consciousness of sin. Sin consciousness destroys your faith. That is why the devil is the accuser of the brethren. He likes to bring up your past. He will bring up something you've done or something you should have done that you didn't do!

Did you know that man can never quite measure up? Not just in what he did that he shouldn't have done, but in what he didn't do which he should have done! The devil has always got something to bring up so that you don't quite measure up.

Sin consciousness destroys faith and is a product of religion. However, righteousness consciousness is the product of the Gospel of Jesus Christ. The Gospel of Christ is a revelation of righteousness. That means that as a born-again believer you can stand before God without a sense of sin, guilt, or inferiority.

Everybody runs just a little bit of a guilt temperature. Guilt says, "I didn't do enough, I should have done, could have done, or wish I would have done!" Psychologists say that if they could just get rid of guilt, they would get rid of 80% of their patients!

The source of depression and most mental problems is a sense of guilt or shame. No matter what happened, whether it was your fault or someone else's, the devil will somehow manage to make sure you feel bad about it. It may be things or people that you don't even know. The devil is constantly trying to produce guilt because sin consciousness destroys faith.

Not Guilty

Sin consciousness makes you not want to talk to God because you know, He knows, we know, and everybody knows! You might think, "I don't want to pray," because you feel like you are disqualified or unworthy. You really have no expectation of His blessing. Sin consciousness leaves you in a state of continuing to try to be accepted by God, but the Gospel brings you into a state of perfect standing with God. This does not happen based on what you have done, but based on what Jesus did with His blood.

> *Sin consciousness destroys faith and is a product of religion. However, righteousness consciousness is the product of the Gospel of Jesus Christ.*

Psychologists say that in a threat environment, communication is corrupted. In other words, in order to establish clear communication, the threat has to be removed. Guilt and shame leave you feeling unworthy and with no confidence towards God. In order to restore us to perfect fellowship with Him, God had to prove His love for us in that while we were yet sinners Christ died for us (Romans 5:8). Through the blood of Jesus, the blood of His cross, clear communication was established. God had to do something to remove the guilt and produce a righteousness consciousness in you so that you can be restored to perfect fellowship with Him.

Very few people ever accept and receive this kind of righteousness. The moment you understand that you have been made the righteousness of God in Christ, your faith immediately takes off to a supernatural level. Then you can say, "I expect God's best blessings because I am right with God!"

Who shall lay any thing to the charge of God's elect? It is God that justifieth. Who is he that condemneth? It is Christ that died, yea rather, that is risen again, who is even at the right hand of God, who also maketh intercession for us.

~ ***Romans 8:33,34***

Who can bring up charges against you now? It is God that justifies. In other words, because of the blood of Jesus and His righteousness, the highest court in the land has declared you *not guilty*! You have not only been declared *not guilty*, but all the charges have also been dropped!

Free From Shame

Human behavior is interesting. Have you ever sat at the mall and watched people for an hour? It is very entertaining. Why do they dress the way they do, poke holes in their bodies, and pull crazy stunts? It is always interesting to watch people and wonder why they do what they do.

> *The blood of Jesus cleanses our conscience from guilt and shame. Shame is at the root of all self-defeating behavior.*

Here is what Christian psychologists, Minirth and Meier, have to say about human behavior: *Shame is at the root of all self-defeating behavior.* When people begin to feel worthless, they really don't need the devil to kill them, they will kill themselves. These psychologists go on to say, "Anytime that you find an addiction — whether it is an eating addiction, drug addiction, spending addiction, or approval addiction—you will always find shame." Shame is at the root of all addiction.

How are you going to get rid of the shame? If the Gospel of Jesus Christ can get rid of the root of shame in your life, then it can change your behavior. Faith in the blood of Jesus will bring a righteousness consciousness that will change the total direction of your life. It will change the way you think and the way you talk. Through faith in the blood, everything changes. It will set you *completely* free. He whom the Son sets free is free indeed!

I Went to Jail

When I was 17 years old, some of my friends and I skipped school and took off in my '55 Chevrolet. We went riding on the beach dunes down in south Texas. While we were jumping the dunes, I had one guy on top of the car, one on the hood, and one on the back of this old '55 Chevrolet. My friends were flying all over and off of the car! Who knows what a nut can do when they're 17 years old! We were just having a big time!

We were way down the beach towards Galveston when we found an old beach house. We were going to have us a party! So we broke into that beach house and my friends said, "Man, look at this! Let's load this stuff up!" Now, my dad was a pastor, so I said, "We'll have some fun in here but you all ain't gonna steal nothin'!" What I was doing was wrong anyway, but I wasn't going to let them steal anything and put it in my car!

So we are in there having a party and guess who pulls up? A Texas Ranger! To make a long story short, he took us all to jail! Because I was 17 years old, I was treated as an adult and had charges brought against me.

You can probably imagine what happened next. I had to call my momma from the county jail. I said, "Mom, you need to come get me." She said, "Where are you?" I said, "Well, I'm in jail." She said, "Prop your feet up and stay awhile. It's Wednesday and we have church tonight!" So that's what I did. About midnight, my dad and four deacons came and got me out of jail. Now I'm in trouble... lots of trouble! I felt bad about myself and for my dad. Three of the deacons were looking at me like they wanted to kill me!

One of those deacons used to be the meanest man in town. He had just gotten saved and filled with the Holy Spirit. While we were in the elevator, he put his hand on my shoulder and said, "Mark, you're gonna be alright." I thought it was amazing that he would speak those words of faith because I didn't think I was going to be alright.

> *In Christ, there is no record that you ever did anything wrong. Not only are you forgiven, but you have been made the righteousness of God in Christ.*

Well, my Dad ended up sending me to east Africa to spend three months with a missionary. There was no rock-n-roll music, no '55 Chevrolet, no girlfriends — as a matter of fact, no friends at all! I worked with a missionary who would go way out in the bush. We would stay out there and listen to hyenas howl at night and elephants grunt. During those three months, I spent all of my time in the Word, and the Lord began to change my life.

Drop the Charges

My dad dealt with the situation and the authorities ended up dropping the charges. When I found out they had dropped the charges, I was really happy. I am telling you, I was happy!

Several years ago, I went to Canada to go deer hunting. I went up to Saskatchewan to get myself a trophy buck.

While going through customs, the officials pulled up my information on their computer and asked me if I had ever been arrested. I said, "No, I've never been arrested." Then I said, "Well, I was arrested when I was 17." They said, "We've got that on your record right here." I said, "Yeah, but they dropped the charges." They looked at me suspiciously so I said, "What do I need to do about this?" They said, "The charges may have been dropped, but it is still on your record. You need to get a lawyer and get your record *expunged.*"

When I came home from that trip, I got a lawyer in Texas so that my record could be expunged. It took about a year, but now when they bring up my name, the charges have been completely cleared from my record. Now, I am really happy because I recently went moose hunting in Canada and when they pulled up my name—there was nothing there!

Your Record Has Been Cleared

I was happy when the charges were dropped, but I am a lot happier knowing there is no record that the charges were ever there! Most people don't completely understand forgiveness. They might believe that God can drop the charges, but they are not convinced that their record has been cleared. Jesus did more than forgive you when He made you righteous; He made you a brand new creation. Old things are passed away and everything has become new!

> *Therefore if any man be in Christ, he is a new creature: old things are passed away; behold, all things are become new.*
>
> ~ *2 Corinthians 5:17*

What God did for you in Christ is more than just dropping the charges. In Christ, there is no record that you ever did anything wrong. Not only are you forgiven, but you have been made the righteousness of God in Christ. The charges have been dropped and your record has been cleared! There are no consequences! This righteousness is a gift. There is nothing you could have done to earn it! If anybody wants to bring up charges, the situation has already been dealt with at the highest level. God declares you righteous — that's the highest court in the land!

A Revelation of Righteousness

And be found in him, not having mine own righteousness, which is of the law, but that which is through the faith

> *of Christ, the righteousness which is of God by faith.*
>
> ~ *Philippians 3:9*

God made Jesus to be sin for us that we might be made the righteousness of God in Him (2 Corinthians 5:21). The Gospel is a revelation of righteousness (Romans 1:16-17). You can never be more righteous than the day you confessed Jesus Christ as your Lord because He gave you His righteousness. You can grow in faith, in love, and in the fruit of the Spirit—but you cannot grow in righteousness. Righteousness is a state of being that restores you into perfect fellowship with God without a sense of sin, guilt, or inferiority.

As a Pharisee, Paul did everything by the law. He did everything right, trying to produce his own righteousness, but he still could not produce it. To some religious people it sounds like heresy when you say, "I have been made the righteousness of God in Christ." Religion wants to try to motivate people by guilt and condemnation. They think that if they tell people that they have been made righteous, they will quit coming to church. It really does just the opposite in you. Grace produces a desire to serve God.

First Class Righteousness

Trina and I travel a lot and have flown in economy class, business class, and first class. I have noticed that there is a great deal of difference between the service in first class and economy class.

When you get on the plane in first class, the attendants will immediately make sure you have everything to make you comfortable. They will take your coat, make sure you have a blanket or pillow, and help you put up your belongings. You are offered something to drink or eat and they call you by your name. "Mr. Hankins, what would you like to eat? Beef or chicken?" They will even bring out a hot fudge sundae if you want one!

> *There is no economy class righteousness.*
> *All of the God-kind of righteousness is*
> *first class righteousness!*

However, in economy class, you are just in the back. They almost act irritated that you are there! You've got someone sitting next to you with their shoes off and their feet stink, and their kids are crawling over the seats. The seating isn't so comfortable and you better not ask for anything special — they'll tell you to get it yourself! If you have an aisle seat, you can look up the aisle and see into first class. You know things are much better up there, but you are stuck in economy class. After a while, they won't even let you look. They pull a curtain, as if to say that you don't even deserve to look into first class! You develop a real economy class mentality as the person next to you goes to sleep, snoring and slobbering!

God spoke to me through all of this and said, "There is no *economy class* righteousness! All of the God-kind of righteousness is *first class* righteousness!" There are some people who don't know about first class righteousness so they go ahead and go to the back of the plane. But the moment you received Jesus, you were made the righteousness of God.

You are heirs of God and joint-heirs with Jesus Christ (Romans 8:17). You reign as kings in life because of God's grace and the gift of righteousness (Romans 5:17). When you come on board in Christ, all of Heaven stands at attention. The blessings of Heaven are yours in Him. The authority of Heaven is yours in His name. God is your very own Father and you are His very own child.

God's Great Reach

The blood reaches the highest place in Heaven and the deepest place in your heart. The precious blood of Jesus is applied in Heaven and in our hearts. His blood cleanses us from all sin. Just as Smith Wigglesworth said, "There is not one thing in me the blood does not cleanse." The blood removes the stain of sin and produces a righteousness consciousness. Now we have confidence before God and confidence in life. Our faith is strong in His blood.

Confession of Faith

- I have been justified freely by the grace of Jesus (Romans 3:24).

- Because I am made righteous, I am filled with quietness and peace (Isaiah 32:17).

- When the enemy brings accusations against me, I know that I am not guilty because it is God who justifies me (Romans 8:33).

- I am in Christ and share His righteousness by faith (Philippians 3:9).

THE BLOOD
POWER TO
DRAW NEAR

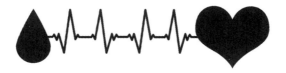

LET US DRAW NEAR WITH A TRUE HEART IN FULL
ASSURANCE OF FAITH, HAVING OUR HEARTS
SPRINKLED FROM AN EVIL CONSCIENCE, AND
OUR BODIES WASHED WITH PURE WATER.
~ HEBREWS 10:22

When we exercise our right of access to God, it gives God access to our lives and our needs.

~ *Mark Hankins*

CHAPTER 8

Access Granted

Having therefore, brethren, boldness to enter into the holiest by the blood of Jesus, By a new and living way, which he hath consecrated for us, through the veil, that is to say, his flesh; And having an high priest over the house of God; Let us draw near with a true heart in full assurance of faith, having our hearts sprinkled from an evil conscience, and our bodies washed with pure water.

~ *Hebrews 10:19-22*

I have a friend who was able to get a picture with former president Ronald Reagan. When he showed me the picture I said, "Is this a joke?" He said, "No. I was actually in his office." I said, "Who took you in there?"

I asked him this question because I knew he did not get himself in to see Ronald Reagan! Then he told me that he knew someone who let him in. The only reason that he had access to the president was because someone else had brought him in! The word *access* is defined by William Barclay in his book *New Testament Words* as:

1. Bringing chosen men into the presence of God that they may be ordained as priests for His worship and his service

2. The bringing of someone into the presence of something specially sacred and holy

3. Introducing a person into the presence of some higher authority

4. Introducing a person into the presence of royalty

Every definition of access implies the introduction of someone. This is exactly what Jesus did for us. Barclay goes on to say, "Jesus is the person who introduces us into the royal presence of God." *Noah Webster's 1828 Dictionary* defines *access* as:

1. A coming to; near approach; admittance; admission, as to gain access to royalty

2. Approach or the way by which a thing may be approached; as, the access is by a neck of land
3. Means of approach; liberty to approach; implying previous obstacles

Hindrances Removed

One of the definitions of *access* implies that previous hindrances have been removed in order to have liberty to approach. The veil in the temple was torn when Jesus died. Hebrews 10:20 says, "...through the veil, that is to say, his flesh." According to this verse, the veil that blocked the entrance into the Holy of Holies was the body of Jesus. When His flesh was torn we were granted access into Christ—into the Holy of Holies.

God sees us in Christ. Access through the veil (His flesh) gives us access into Christ, which is the same thing as seeing yourself through the blood. It is synonymous with faith in the blood.

For through Him we both have access by one Spirit unto the Father.

~ Ephesians 2:18

...we actually enjoy our access to the Father through Him.

> ~ *Ephesians 2:18 (Hudson)*

...for through him, we both possess the right of access through the one Spirit to the Father.

> ~ *Ephesians 2:18 (Barclay)*

In whom we have boldness and access with confidence by the faith of him.

> ~ *Ephesians 3:12*

In Whom, because of our faith in Him, we dare to have the boldness (courage and confidence) of free access (an unreserved approach to God with freedom and without fear).

> ~ *Ephesians 3:12 (AMP)*

Through faith in the blood of Jesus, we are granted access into closest fellowship with the Father God. We have been granted access and admission into the presence of royalty in Christ. Our faith in Jesus literally brings us before Him. When we exercise our right of access to God, it gives God access to our lives and our needs.

By whom also we have access by faith into this grace wherein we stand, and rejoice in hope of the glory of God.

~ *Romans 5:2*

Through Him also we have [our] access (entrance, introduction) by faith into this grace (state of God's favor)...

~ *Romans 5:2 (AMP)*

By faith we access His grace. We are the believers and He is the performer. Let us exercise our right of access and come before Him whom we believe. We can expect great results as our faith is strong in the Lord.

Free From Sin

But if we walk in the light, as he is in the light, we have fellowship one with another, and the blood of Jesus Christ his Son cleanseth us from all sin.

~ *1 John 1:7*

You will enter into a realm of illumination, a realm of revelation by the power of the Holy Spirit. He reveals the preciousness and the power of the blood of Christ. I

*have found by the revelation of the Spirit that there is
not one thing in me that the blood does not cleanse (1
John 1:9). I have found that God sanctifies me by the
blood and reveals the effectiveness of His works by the
Spirit.*

~ *Smith Wigglesworth*

Although sin may try to damage you, reaching all the
way into the very fabric of your personality, the blood of
Jesus has a far greater reach. It cleanses us completely
and removes every trace of the stain that sin leaves. Not
only does the blood remove sin, but it also removes sin
consciousness.

> *Although sin may try to damage you, reaching
> all the way into the very fabric
> of your personality, the blood of Jesus
> has a far greater reach.*

I am reminded of something that happened during our
family vacation a few years ago. We decided to drive
through a wild animal park in Oklahoma. We purchased
some small buckets of feed to give to the various animals
as we drove though the park. My daughter, Alicia, was

sitting in the front passenger seat. My wife, Trina, and my son, Aaron, were sitting in the back seat.

At first, we saw only deer. We fed them, and they were nice and cute. Then a llama came strolling up on Alicia's side of the van. He scared her so much that she quickly rolled up her window.

I laughed and said, "I'm not afraid of a llama." The llama must have heard me say that because immediately he came to my side of the van. I began to feed him out of my bucket. All of a sudden, he forced his whole head in the window and ate out of my bucket with his whole head in my lap. Alicia and I began to laugh nervously. Then the llama pulled his head out of the bucket and sneezed in my van. Llama spit, snot, and slimy stuff went all over the van and on our clothes. It was so nasty and had a horrible smell. I immediately slapped the llama's head to get him out and rolled up the window, but it was too late—the damage had been done.

We left the park and headed for the nearest store to get something to clean up the mess. We finally got the slime out, but the smell was more difficult. During our whole vacation we could smell the llama sneeze every time we got in the van. That smell stayed in the van for months before we finally got it out. The llama was long gone, but the smell was still there.

> *Being a Christian is more than just having your sins forgiven — you become a new person in Christ.*

The same way the llama left a smell that we couldn't get out, the devil will try to stick his head in your life and leave a mess that stays with you. Praise God, we can apply the blood of Jesus and be cleansed from sin and all its effects. The blood of Jesus not only removes the evidence that you sinned, but it also gets rid of the consciousness and the smell of sin.

See Yourself Supernaturally

God wants you to see yourself supernaturally not after your natural identity, but after your supernatural identity. You must have a change of identity before you can reach your divine destiny. In 2 Corinthians 5:16,17, Paul says, "Wherefore henceforth know we no man after the flesh... Therefore if any man be in Christ, he is a new creature: old things are passed away; behold, all things are become new." Paul is talking about believers. He is saying that as Christians, we don't see or know ourselves naturally.

Sometimes as believers, we never really get to know ourselves supernaturally. We just continue to see ourselves naturally. But Paul said, "If any man be *in Christ....*" Many times people talk about what they are trying to be, what they ought to be, what they are someday going to be, but they never actually determine what they be! You need to settle who you are and what you have in Christ right now! You are not trying to be — you are right now *in Christ!*

A New Species of Being

Therefore if any man be in Christ, he is a new creature...

~ *2 Corinthians 5:17*

The word *new* in this scripture means "new in kind or new in quality." It literally means "unheard of before." When you got born again, you became a new creation in Christ. You became new in kind or new in quality. Some translations say, "a new species of being that never existed before." In other words, being a Christian is more than just having your sins forgiven — you become a new person in Christ.

Notice that it says "if any person is in Christ," not "if any person is in church." You can be in church and not be *in Christ*. Paul uses the terminology *in Christ, new creation, unheard of before, new in kind, a new kind of a person,* so that there would be no doubt that you understand that you are a new person *in Christ*. You are such a different person in Christ, that you need someone to introduce you to your new self!

I would like to introduce you to your new self. You may still think you are who you used to be, taking your personality from things that run in your family naturally. But if you have been born again, you have been born of God. You need to find out what runs in your new family because God is your Father and Jesus is your older Brother! This means you have the same life, the same power, the same ability, and the same righteousness as Jesus. You've been born again with it! God says you are a new creature—a new creation in Christ.

Eternal Life

That if thou shalt confess with thy mouth the Lord Jesus, and shalt believe in thine heart that God hath raised him from the dead, thou shalt be saved.

~ ***Romans 10:9***

He that hath the Son hath life; and he that hath not the Son of God hath not life.

~ *1 John 5:12*

Are you saved? The Greek word for "saved" is *sozo*, which means *safety, deliverance, healing, preservation, and soundness.* When you got saved, you were delivered from the power of darkness. When you made Jesus the Lord of your life, you received eternal life.

The gift of God is eternal life. Eternal life is not just life that goes on forever. The word *eternal* literally refers to the life of God because God is the only true eternal being.

For as the Father hath life in himself; so hath he given to the Son to have life in himself.

~ *John 5:26*

Jesus said that the Father God has life in Himself. The life in God is eternal life. *Eternal life* could better be translated as "the life of the Eternal One." Jesus said, "I came to give you eternal life — the life of God."

The Greek word *zoe* means "the God kind of life." This is referring to a quality of life, not just something that you obtain when you die! It is something you get when you make Jesus the Lord of your life. He gives you the gift of eternal life which is the life of God. The life that is in God, the life that is in Christ, the life of Heaven, and the life that raised Christ from the dead is the same life that is in you!

Have you received eternal life? This life in you will quicken your spirit, give illumination to your mind, and get into your bone marrow, causing healing to come into your body. Say this now: "I have received eternal life!"

A Man in Christ

This life which flows from God into man is something totally different from anything experienced on the natural plane. It is different not only in degree, but also in kind. It is a different kind of life. It is supernatural life. It makes a man a new creation. It is not the intensification of powers already possessed but the sudden emergence of an entirely new and original element. When a man comes to be in Christ, he begins to live in the post-resurrection life of Christ. The life that he now lives bears the quality of eternity.

~ **A Man In Christ** *by James Stewart*

When you got born again, you were "in Christ-ed." You are in Him, so whatever is in Him is in you. The life of God is now in you. In Christ, you now have access to Heaven itself and to the very life of God!

Eternal life refers to the quality of the life, not the duration of the life. When you made Jesus the Lord of your life, the same life that overcame at the resurrection came into your spirit. Because God has this life in Him, He never loses. God is a champion! He wins every time!

> *The same life that is in God, the same life that is in Christ, the life of Heaven, and the same life that raised Christ from the dead is the same life that is in you!*

This life of God will do the same for you. It will get rid of your losing mentality. You cannot have a failure mentality and have the God kind of life because God expects to win in every situation, in every challenge, and in every battle.

The life that is in God overflows and comes out in the form of a river all over Heaven—the River of Life. You can just go swim around in the River of Life. There are trees that grow up out of the River of Life. There is healing just in the fruit of these trees.

God overflows with life. He has so much of this life in Him that He radiates with energy and with power. Blessing, love, joy, peace, favor, goodness, and glory — these are all ingredients in the life of God.

...I am come that they might have life, and that they might have it more abundantly.

~ *John 10:10*

God has an unlimited source of this life and one of the reasons for Jesus' coming was not to take you to Heaven but to get Heaven in you. He wanted to make you more than a match for the devil right here in this world. He took the life of God and put that life into your spirit.

Champion in Christ

For whatsoever is born of God overcometh the world: and this is the victory that overcometh the world, even our faith.

~ *1 John 5:4*

When you made Jesus your Lord, you were born again or "re-fathered." In other words, at your first birth you were born into Adam and shared in his condition. But now that you are born again in Christ, you are a different kind of creature that never existed before. You are a thoroughbred. You are a champion in Christ!

Everything that Jesus did in His death, burial, and resurrection, He did for us; it is set to the credit of our account just like we did it. You are in Christ in His death, His burial, His resurrection, and His blessing. God deposited everything He had in Christ, and then placed you in Christ.

Divine Language

The Apostle Paul used the phrases *In Christ, In Him* or *In Whom* over 130 times in the scriptures in order to explain what happened to you when you got saved (born again, received eternal life, made Jesus your Lord). He used this divine language to explain a divine reality. The two words "in Christ" are really blood covenant terminology.

> *Everything that Jesus did in His death, burial, and resurrection, He did for us; it is set to the credit of our account just like we did it.*

Second Corinthians 5:17 says that you are a new creature in Christ. You are now operating in another realm because you've got the life of God and the Spirit of God on the inside of you. You may look like a regular person on the outside, dwelling here on earth, but you actually have access to Heaven. Your spirit is hooked up to Heaven and the life of God is on the inside of you.

> ## *"In Christ" is really blood covenant terminology.*

God created you in Christ, and He deposited into Christ everything He wanted you to be. If you are not impressed with who you are in Christ, you've not seen Him lately! There is an ever increasing understanding and revelation of who you are and what you have in Christ.

After thirty years of ministry, the Apostle Paul said to the Philippian believers, "That I may know Him, and the power of His resurrection, and the fellowship of His sufferings, being made conformable unto his death" (Philippians 3:10). In other words, Paul was saying, "What

I would like to do is just get lost in Him...just to know who I am in Him."

Radical Identity Change

Your destiny is connected to your identity. You cannot reach your destiny without a change of identity. Jacob could never have reached his destiny if he had not become Israel. God changed his identity—He changed his name and therefore changed his identity. Abram did not reach his destiny until he became Abraham. Gideon had to see himself as "a mighty man of valor" before he could reach his destiny.

There has to be a radical identity change or you will revert back to what others may have labeled you. You have to accept God's Word for it—you are who God says you are! Get lost in your new identity of who you are in Christ!

I like this story I heard years ago. There was a guy who suffered from low self-esteem who went to a psychiatrist. The psychiatrist asked him, "What is your problem?" He said, "Well I think I'm a dog." The psychiatrist said, "How long have you had this problem?" The man replied, "Ever since I was a puppy." So the psychiatrist said, "Well, sit down on the couch and let's talk about it." The man quickly replied, "I'm not allowed." As you can see from this story, some people are still dealing with problems they have had since they were puppies. However, if they will accept God's Word, they can have a fresh new start (2 Corinthians 5:17).

Group Picture

Have you ever taken a group picture? What is the first thing you look for in a group picture? Yourself. The reality of your redemption is in the group picture. When you find yourself in the picture of the crucifixion, things aren't looking too good.

> ### *If you are not impressed with who are in Christ, you've not seen Him lately!*

But three days later, the picture changes from the crucifixion to the resurrection. Now you are blessed because you are in Christ in His resurrection. Now you are looking like a champion! Now you are redeemed! Now you are healed! When He sat down, you were seated with Him in that place of dominion and authority. Now you are *in Christ*!

I am crucified with Christ: nevertheless I live; yet not I, but Christ liveth in me: and the life which I now live in the flesh I live by the faith of the Son of God, who loved me, and gave himself for me.

~ *Galatians 2:20*

...Christ took me to the cross with Him, and I died there with Him.

~ *Galatians 2:20 (Laubach)*

I identified myself completely with Him...

~ *Galatians 2:20 (MSG)*

I consider myself as having died and now enjoying a second existence, which is simply Jesus using my body.

~ *Galatians 2:20 (Distilled)*

The death, burial, and resurrection of Christ is a group picture. The Pauline epistles tell us that we were crucified with Christ. We died with Him; we were buried and made alive with Him; we were raised up together and seated with Him. The four Gospels (Matthew, Mark, Luke, and John) show us what man saw. Paul's letters reveal to us what God saw!

A Royal Priesthood

But ye are a chosen generation, a royal priesthood, an
holy nation, a peculiar people; that ye should shew forth
the praises of him who hath called you out of darkness
into his marvellous light.

~ 1 Peter 2:9

You are a priest with a royal lineage. Royalty runs in
your family. As a king, you reign in life through one man,
Jesus Christ!

...Unto him that loved us, and washed us from our sins
in his own blood, And hath made us kings and priests
unto God and his Father; to him be glory and dominion
for ever and ever. Amen.

~ *Revelation 1:5,6*

In the Old Testament, only the priest had access into
the Holy of Holies and the presence of God. In the New
Testament, everybody in the Body of Christ has access
to the Holy of Holies and can call God, "Father." Smith
Wigglesworth said, "You need to see how wonderful you
are in God and how helpless you are in yourself." You will
find the answers to your problems when you realize that
you are a new creature in Christ. You have been granted

access into the very presence of God! From that place, you can get victory in every area of your life!

Confession of Faith

- I have boldness to enter the Holiest by the blood of Jesus (Hebrews 10:19).

- I draw near to God with full assurance of faith (Hebrews 10:22).

- I have access by one Spirit to the Father (Ephesians 2:18).

- I have access with confidence by faith in God (Ephesians 3:12).

- I have access by faith into this grace wherein I stand (Romans 5:2).

- I am a new creature and am the very righteousness of God in Christ (2 Corinthians 5:17,21).

- I have the life of the Son of God in me (1 John 5:12).

- I have the abundant life of God in me because of His blood (John 10:10).

- I am born of God and overcome the world (1 John 5:4).

- It is no longer I that lives, but Christ who lives in me (Galatians 2:20).

- I am a chosen generation, a royal priesthood, a holy nation, a peculiar people (1 Peter 2:9).

So perfect is the reconciliation, and so really has sin been covered and blotted out, that he who believes in Christ is looked upon, and treated by God, as entirely righteous. The acquittal that he has received from God is so complete that there is nothing, absolutely nothing, to prevent him from approaching God with the utmost freedom.

~ Andrew Murray

CHAPTER 9

Before Him

According as he hath chosen us in him before the foundation of the world, that we should be holy and without blame before him in love.

> ~ *Ephesians 1:4*

And Abraham got up early in the morning to the place where he stood before the Lord.

> ~ *Genesis 19:27*

(As it is written, I have made thee a father of many nations,) before him whom he believed, even God, who quickeneth the dead, and calleth those things which be not as though they were.

> ~ *Romans 4:17*

The words *before Him* stood out to me as I studied the steps of the faith of Abraham in Romans 4:17-21. Today, believers all over the world follow in Abraham's footsteps to receive from God. God has not changed and neither has the way faith works. Notice the phrase "before Him whom he believed." The words *before Him* are also translated "in His presence" or "in His sight." Abraham's faith was loaded with the presence of God. He was God-conscious. I like to say that some people are self-conscious, some people are people-conscious, some people are devil-conscious, some people are time-conscious, and some people are unconscious! However, to win the fight of faith, we must be God-conscious!

God-Conscious Faith

Abraham had a habit of praying and standing *before the Lord*. He did not just have the promises of God, he also had the presence of God. He stood "before Him whom he believed." Abraham knew how to fellowship with God and practiced standing in the presence of God. He did not just know the Word of God; he knew the God of the Word. Abraham was a friend of God. He communed with God.

Let us not stand at a distance as if God were inaccessible;
but on the contrary, let us draw near with a sincere
and affectionate heart, in the full assurance of faith,
supported by such considerations as these, which may
well embolden us...to make our approach unto Him in
the most cheerful expectation of His blessing.

~   *Hebrews 10:22 (Doddridge)*

Sometimes it seems that believers today try to win the faith fight without getting before God. They quote scriptures but don't seem to know how to access the presence of God. They try to believe without getting before Him. Some believers try to believe at a distance. However, there is no such thing as long distance faith. We must draw near...close to the heart of God and believe in His presence (Hebrews 10:19-23).

Reconcile Your Heart

But rather, you have come to Mount Zion, even to the
city of the living God, the heavenly Jerusalem, and
to countless multitudes of angels in festal gathering,
And to the church (assembly) of the Firstborn who are
registered [as citizens] in heaven, and to the God Who

> *is Judge of all, and to the spirits of the righteous (the redeemed in heaven) who have been made perfect.*
>
> ~   *Hebrews 12:22,23 (AMP)*

Faith in the blood of Jesus will bring you into the reality of Heaven itself. It will bring you into the presence of God. God desires for you to respond to His invitation to enter into His presence. Don't allow religion or guilt to stop you from coming before Him. The blood has been applied in Heaven.

Reconcile your heart to the reality of redemption. Have faith in His blood. His blood alone has done everything that is necessary for you to come before Him and enjoy the benefits of redemption.

The comers are those who make their approach unto God. Instead of following a type or shadow, they are making their way into the reality of redemption. The redemption that Jesus paid for with real blood gives real answers for real problems! I am not talking about playing church for an hour and going back into the real world. No! We enter into the real realm of God, receive real answers, real strength, real direction and come out with a real blessing!

Fellowship With God

It is interesting when my kids come to my house because there is no telling what will be missing when they leave. As my children, they know they have access to my provision. I tell them to get whatever they want, and if they like something in particular, I try to have plenty of it. Why? Because I am their dad. My desire is to always bless my children.

> *God did not create us just to have a relationship with us; He created us for fellowship.*

It is the same thing with God. God doesn't want us coming to Him begging. He's our Father and there is no limit to His provision for us. God did not create us just to have a relationship with us; He created us for fellowship.

O God, thou art my God; early will I seek thee: my soul thirsteth for thee, my flesh longeth for thee in a dry and thirsty land, where no water is. To see thy power and thy glory, so as I have seen thee in the sanctuary. Because thy loving-kindness is better than life, my lips shall praise thee. Thus will I bless thee while I live: I will lift up my hands in thy name. My soul shall be satisfied as with marrow and fatness; and my mouth shall praise thee with joyful lips.

~   *Psalm 63:1-5*

Another translation says, "I am satisfied like someone who has just had a feast." The moment you get into the presence of God, you will be satisfied. He is more than enough for you. He will take care of every facet of your life. Your satisfaction is not based on what you have or don't have but on your fellowship with God.

> *All low grade faith comes from a low grade of fellowship with God.*
>
> *- E.W. Kenyon*

When two people get married, they immediately have a relationship with one another. However, relationship alone does not make a strong union. They might call each other husband and wife and live in the same house, but that does not mean they know each other's desires.

Fellowship — time spent with one another — is what makes their relationship grow and their marriage strong.

It is the same with God. You may call God your Father, but that does not mean you have spent time with Him to learn His desires. When you fellowship with God, your faith in Him grows strong. E. W. Kenyon said, "All low grade faith comes from a low grade of fellowship with God." Out of rich fellowship with God comes a faith that enables you to see things from a supernatural perspective and opens the door to possibilities. You come out of His presence with a bold confession of faith that moves mountains.

Come Unto Me

Let us therefore come boldly unto the throne of grace, that we may obtain mercy, and find grace to help in time of need.

~ *Hebrews 4:16*

Reverend Kenneth E. Hagin (Dad Hagin) tells about having a vision of Jesus Christ. When he saw the Lord, the first thing he did was fall down at Jesus' feet and say,

"Lord, no one as unworthy as I am should look upon Your face." He said that Jesus then upended all of his theology. He said that he had a truckload of unworthiness and sense of guilt and shame. Jesus said, "Stand up on your feet for I have made you worthy." He said that he was then standing face to face with Jesus.

And the Spirit and the bride say, Come. And let him that heareth say, Come. And let him that is athirst come. And whosoever will, let him take the water of life freely.

~ *Revelation 22:17*

Come unto me, all ye that labour and are heavy laden, and I will give you rest.

~ *Matthew 11:28*

The law could not make the comers or worshippers perfect because they had a sense of failure and guilt. They desired to come into the presence of God but the law would not allow it. Sacrifices were offered year after year, but they could not effectively deal with man's problem or condition, which had isolated him from the presence of God.

But when Jesus came, He said, "...Lo, I come...to do thy will, O God" (Hebrews 10:7). The law could not make the worshippers perfect, but through one offering, Jesus has made forever perfect those that are sanctified. Jesus made the perfect sacrifice to restore perfect fellowship with God.

For by one offering he hath perfected for ever them that are sanctified.

~ *Hebrews 10:14*

So with that one sacrifice He made us holy and brought us into perfect union with God.

~ *Hebrews 10:14 (Laubach)*

For by one sacrifice, valid forever, he enabled men to enter into perfect communion with God.

~ *Hebrews 10:14 (Barclay)*

...He has forever qualified those who are purified from sin to approach God.

~ *Hebrews 10:14 (Goodspeed)*

God's plan was to produce a perfect fellowship through the blood of Jesus where worshippers could come into His presence. Hebrews 10:10 says, "By the which will we are sanctified through the offering of the body of Jesus Christ once for all." The blood of Jesus has the power to produce a consciousness free from sin. Jesus said, "Come." We have to take the initiative to come before His throne of grace.

The Greatest Privilege

Now we may walk right into the very Holy of Holies where God is, because of the blood of Jesus.

~ Hebrews 10:19 (TLB)

Let us as members of His family, exercise our right of access and press closer and closer to the Father. But we must come with childlike faith and the unshakeable assurance that He is eager to receive us.

~ Hebrews 10:22 (Lovett)

The greatest privilege and highest calling of every believer is to fellowship with God our Father and with the Lord Jesus Christ. Many Christians have substituted duty for fellowship. God desires fellowship with you more than anything in the world.

It is never a waste of time to stop at a filling station for fuel when you are on a long trip. The same is true spiritually. Just a few moments in His presence saves time. He fills us with His strength, wisdom, peace, and joy. John Wesley said, "It seems that God is limited by our prayer life. He can do nothing for humanity unless someone asks Him." Someone said it this way, "Every failure in life is a prayer failure." Prayer is the greatest business transaction in the world.

> *The greatest privilege and highest calling of every believer is to fellowship with God our Father and with the Lord Jesus Christ. Many Christians have substituted duty for fellowship.*

We must have a daily prayer habit. Time with Him changes everything. One hour in His presence can restore years. E.W. Kenyon said, "Force yourself into the prayer life. Regardless of how you feel, drive yourself to prayer."

You see, prayer has several elements. It brings you into personal fellowship and touch with the Father, and with the Holy Spirit, and with Jesus. All three of the Godhead are brought into the prayer life. You are praying to the Father. You are praying in the Name of Jesus. You are praying through the Holy Spirit. Your prayer is based upon the Word. It brings this earth heart of ours into contact with the heavenly center of all divine power and activity. You can't spend any length of time in prayer without being affected by it. The quietness, the unshaken faith, the deep, unsounded peace that pervades the Godhead, will overflow into the pray-er's life. Said an anxious and nervous mother: "You will have to forgive me, children, but I forgot to visit the Master this morning, and so I lack His quietness and His strength." Many of us can make that confession, that our irritability, weakness, and lack of spiritual insight comes from not sitting in the presence of the Master. One cannot spend an hour in conscious communion with the Father, the Son, the Spirit and the Word without carrying away from that trysting place the fragrance about Jesus that lingers with the pray-ers. They are slow to speak. They are slow to judge. They are quick to love and quick to help. There is a holy calmness about their lives that challenges the restless ones; they crave that quietness of spirit. Again, we cannot spend time with them without partaking of their stability and their unshakableness. One who is easily disturbed, and who in the jolts of life is unseated, will find a new strength and steadiness that will make him a blessing to the world, by spending just a little time with the Rock of our Strength.

~ *E.W. Kenyon*

The "blood faith" grants us access to Heaven's economy and resources.

The Lord Jesus has made a new and living way into the presence of God with His own blood. As we exercise faith in His blood, we are carried right into the presence of the Father (Romans 3:25). The "blood faith" grants us access to Heaven's economy and resources.

Welcome to God's Economy

Welcome to God's economy. Welcome to Heaven's resources. Angels are everywhere on assignment. The voice of the blood of Jesus speaks of mercy. We come boldly to the throne of grace to receive mercy and to find grace to help in the time of need (Hebrews 4:16).

> *But ye are come unto Mount Zion, and unto the city of the living God, the heavenly Jerusalem, and to an innumerable company of angels, to the general assembly and church of the firstborn, which are written in heaven, and to God the Judge of all, and to the spirits of just men made perfect, and to Jesus the mediator of the new covenant, and to the blood of sprinkling, that speaketh better things than that of Abel.*
>
> ~   *Hebrews 12:22-24*

God has given us a personal V.I.P. invitation. We are encouraged to come. Come and find rest because His yoke is easy (Matthew 11:28-30). Come and drink (John 7:37-39; Revelation 22:17). We have been washed in the precious blood of Jesus, and He has made us kings and priests (Revelation 1:5,6). As priests, we have access into His presence. As kings, we rule and reign in life. A priest never went into the presence of God just for himself; he always went into the presence of God to get something for somebody else!

Possession With Intent to Distribute

The captain of the local police narcotics division is a member of our church. One day he said, "Pastor, I want to take you around town." So we went on patrol, and as we drove around town, he explained the local drug activity to me. He showed me all the main trafficking areas for drugs. We even made one drug bust!

The people he caught were crying and angry. I got to talk to them about Jesus while they were on the side of the road. Then I saw the bottle of crack cocaine he found on them. The officer said, "Do you see that? There's enough in that bottle to show they are not just users, but they are distributors." The sentence would be lighter if they only had enough for them to use personally. But because they had a large amount, now it is called "possession with the intent to distribute."

> *Every failure in life is a prayer failure.*

Anytime you get caught in a difficult situation, you ought to have enough faith and enough power from the presence of God that the devil says, "It is clear that they are not just users. They have so much faith that they must have possession with the intent to distribute!" In other words, they have enough faith to bless someone else! They are planning on taking this and passing it out to their family, their children, and their neighborhood!

> *God sees me holy and unblameable, washed in the blood, and blessed with every spiritual blessing!*

The same faith that set you free will set them free. You have possession with the intent to distribute. You ought to say, "I'm guilty. I've been caught with so much faith in the blood of Jesus that I was planning on distributing. I was planning on winning souls and telling people about Jesus so that, through faith in the blood of Jesus, they could be launched out of the atmosphere of sin and death into the presence of God. We were redeemed not with silver and gold, but with the precious blood of Jesus as of a lamb without blemish and without spot.

In His Presence

God created all of us to live in His presence. Sin and Satan came in and we were exiled from the presence of God. Faith in the blood of Jesus brings us right back before Him, bold and unashamed, expecting to receive from Him.

Meeting with God is no small thing. If you have access to God, then somebody had to bring you in. Jesus Christ gives us access and brings us in with His credentials before God. Someone might ask you, "How did you get to have a meeting with God?" You can say, "I have access through the blood of Jesus Christ. I meet with God every day. He sees me holy and unblameable, washed in the blood, and blessed with every spiritual blessing!"

He has his own human body, and now as a result Christ has brought you into the very presence of God, and you are standing there before him with nothing left against you – nothing left that he could even chide you for.

~ Colossians 1:22 (TLB)

You go to church to meet with God but you can also meet with God at your house. Just take 60 minutes and tell your husband, wife, and friends, "Don't call me for the next sixty minutes because I plan on meeting with God. When you meet with God, you will learn, listen, receive and come out with your body feeling well, money coming in, and the direction of God for your life. Just say, "Excuse me, I've got to meet with God!"

In Christ, God has chosen us to stand *before Him*. We are standing in His presence holy and without blame because of His love for us. He is our Father and we are His children. God's plan has always been for us to live *in His presence*. Through faith in the blood of Jesus, we are brought before Him. We are granted access into the closest fellowship with the Father God because of Jesus. Now our faith is loaded with His presence, promise, and power!

Confession of Faith

- I come to Mt. Zion and to God, the Judge of all (Hebrews 12:20-23).

- My flesh longs for God as in a dry and thirsty land where no water is (Psalm 63:1).

- I come boldly to the throne of grace to obtain mercy and find grace to help in the time of need (Hebrews 4:16).

- My spirit is thirsty so I come and drink of the water of life freely (Revelation 22:17).

- I come to Jesus and He gives me rest (Matthew 11:28).

- By the blood, I enter into perfect communion with God (Hebrews 10:14).

- I walk into the Holy of Holies because of the blood of Jesus (Hebrews 10:19).

- The Lord Jesus has made a new and living way into the presence of God with His own blood. The blood of Jesus has the power to cleanse me from sin consciousness. As I exercise faith in His blood, I am carried right into the presence of the Father (Romans 3:25).

- In His presence I am cleansed and find rest for my soul. This "blood faith" grants me access to Heaven's economy and resources. I plan on winning souls and telling people about Jesus so that, through faith in the blood of Jesus, they can be launched out of the atmosphere of sin and death into the presence of God. I am redeemed not with silver and gold, but with the precious blood of Jesus, the Lamb without spot or blemish. In Christ, God has chosen me to stand before Him. I am standing in His presence holy and without blame because of His love for me. He is my Father and I am His child. God's plan has always been for me to live in His presence. Through faith in the blood of Jesus, I am brought before Him. I am granted access into the closest fellowship with the Father God because of Jesus. Now my faith is loaded with His presence, promise, and power!

You will enter into a realm of illumination, a realm of revelation by the power of the Holy Spirit. He reveals the preciousness and the power of the blood of Christ. I have found by the revelation of the Spirit that there is not one thing in me that the blood does not cleanse (1 John 1:9). I have found that God sanctifies me by the blood and reveals the effectiveness of His works by the Spirit.

~ Smith Wigglesworth

CHAPTER 10

Face to Face

Did you know your spirit is longing for more than just a religious experience? You may try to get by with just going to church and doing the normal "Christian" thing, but your heart will never be satisfied until you get into the presence of God and meet with Him. It is in His presence where we find fullness of joy and are changed from the inside out.

Meeting with God requires us to push past our flesh, our feelings, and our mind. When you are in His presence, all other things seem to fade away as you are consumed with Him. You know you are with the Father God, and nothing else matters.

The Bible says that in His presence is fullness of joy (Psalm 16:11). Have you ever noticed someone who has spent time with the Lord all day? They have a smile on their face and a bounce in their step. They have just come from meeting with God, and their hearts are full of joy. When you come face to face with God, your joy tank gets full!

Hearing From God

When we draw closer to God, we are also able to hear His voice more clearly and discern His will and plan for our lives. If you need wisdom and direction, get into His presence. That is where He will talk to you and give you the answers you are seeking.

> ### The closer you come to Him, the easier it is to hear His voice.

I heard a story of an elderly man who thought his wife was going deaf. He decided to test her hearing, so he walked across the room, turned his back, and said, "Can you hear me?" There was no response. So, he backed up a little closer to her and repeated the question, "Can you hear me?" Still there was no response. He backed up again until he was standing near his wife and said, "Can you hear me now?" This time he heard his wife say, "For the third time, I can hear you!" This man thought his wife had a hearing problem, but he was the one going deaf!

If you're having problems hearing from God, then you need to get into His presence. The closer you come to Him, the easier it is to distinguish His voice. If you're struggling with decisions or direction, draw near to God. In His presence, you'll find everything you need.

The Gettin' Place

In Psalm 73, David began to compare himself with the world. Although he was trying to serve God and do the right thing, he ended up looking at the heathens and got frustrated with God. The heathens appeared to be more blessed than David and seemed to be getting ahead of him. However, something happened when David came into the presence of God. Psalm 73:17 says, "Until I went into the sanctuary of God; then understood I their end." David went on to say that the heathens dwell in slippery places, but God is continually with him. In verse 28 David said, "...it is good for me to draw near to God: I have put my trust in the Lord God, that I may declare all thy works."

Spending time in the presence of God is not wasted time. Although we may see others who are not serving God getting ahead in life, we know their end is fruitless. Because we serve the Lord, our end is sure. As we take time to get into God's presence, we receive of His strength, power, and goodness.

When my mother went shopping and bought something new, she would say she got her stuff at "the gettin' place." It didn't matter if it were a new dress, a watch, or some dishes – if you asked her where she got it from, she would simply reply, "At the gettin' place."

> *Joint heir - equal possession because of equal position.*

The presence of God is our "gettin' place." Because we are members of the family of God and have access to His presence, we can come boldly to the throne of grace and receive mercy and grace to help in the time of need.

Whether it's healing, direction, mercy, or strength, we can find it in the presence of God. And if someone asks you where you got it from, you can just say, "I got it from the gettin' place! I've been to the gettin' place, and I know where I can get stuff from!"

Receiving Your Inheritance

When you seek the Lord diligently, God will reward you. In fact, God calls that faith. Hebrews 11:6 in the Amplified Bible says, "…whoever would come near to God must necessarily believe that God exists and that He is the rewarder of those who earnestly and diligently seek Him out." The reward is His inheritance that Paul speaks of in Ephesians 1:18. It has been given out, but we must draw near to receive it.

> *The eyes of your understanding being enlightened; that ye may know what is the hope of his calling, and what the riches of the glory of his inheritance in the saints.*
>
> ~ *Ephesians 1:18*

Not too long ago, I was reading an article in *Forbes* magazine about the 400 billionaires in the United States and observing how they made their money. Some had gotten their wealth through entertainment, oil, or technology. My attention was drawn to three brothers who were worth $3.7 billion each. Next to their names was written "inheritance." They didn't have to do anything to obtain this wealth; they were born into it.

If you're a child of God, then you have "inheritance" written next to your name in Heaven. You didn't have to do anything to get it; you were just born into it.

> *The Spirit itself beareth witness with our spirit, that we are the children of God: And if children, then heirs; heirs of God, and joint-heirs with Christ...*
>
> ~ ***Romans 8:16,17***

> *Giving thanks unto the Father, which hath made us meet to be partakers of the inheritance of the saints in light.*
>
> ~ ***Colossians 1:12***

The dictionary defines *heir* as "equal possession because of equal position." The moment we take our place in God's presence, we are positioning ourselves to receive our inheritance. Because of the shed blood of Jesus, we have a privileged relationship with God — a relationship with an immeasurable inheritance!

A lot of Christians are out of position and not walking in all that the blood has purchased for them. As you draw near to God, take your position in Him and receive your inheritance. Boldly declare everyday, "I take my place in Christ. I take my position!"

Seeking His Face

Although there are many wonderful things we receive in the presence of God, the most precious benefit we receive when we draw near is God Himself. In Psalm 27:8, David wrote about his heart's desire for the presence of God: "When thou saidst, Seek ye my face; my heart said unto thee, Thy face, Lord, will I seek." David just wanted to be with God!

One thing have I desired of the Lord, that will I seek after; that I may dwell in the house of the Lord all the days of my life, to behold the beauty of the Lord, and to enquire in His temple. For in the time of trouble he shall hide me in his pavilion: in the secret of his tabernacle shall he hide me; he shall set me upon a rock. And now my head be lifted up above mine enemies round about

me: therefore will I offer in his tabernacle sacrifices of
joy; I will sing, yea, I will sing praises unto the Lord.

~ **Psalm 27:4-6**

> ## We can get so close to Him that we can't see anything but Him.

Trina and I have been blessed with five precious grandchildren. Gavin, Alicia and Caleb's youngest boy, was born smaller and required some special attention due to health challenges. Since he was so weak, we had to hold Gavin closer and more often than we did the other grandkids. We would hold him tightly, but he would also hold onto us tightly. In fact, we called him Tree Frog because he would latch on to us so closely.

When we held Gavin, he wanted to get as close as he could. Pretty soon, he would be right in our face – forehead to forehead, eyeball to eyeball, nose to nose, mouth to mouth. Even his little hands would have a hold on both ears! He just couldn't get close enough.

Sometimes holding him would get a little messy, but as grandparents, we didn't mind. We actually enjoyed the way he clung to us. When Gavin would get this close to our face, we couldn't see anything but him, and he couldn't see anything but us. While the older grandchildren were outside playing with their toys, Gavin was spending time with us, getting to know the ones who bought the toys.

When we enter the presence of God, we can get so close to Him that we can't see anything but Him. Our focus shifts from all of the "toys" to the Creator of all things. As we draw near, we open our hearts in love towards our Heavenly Father.

> *God is an affectionate Father. He is a lover. Never underestimate His affection for you.*

Many Christians don't understand the affection of the Father God. If we only knew how coming close to Him gives Him such pleasure, we would respond more readily. God is an affectionate Father. He is a lover. Never underestimate His affection for you.

While others are "playing with their toys," let us spend our best time with the Father God. When we seek Him first, everything we need will be added. While the rest of the world is going after wealth, let us go after Him, getting in His face and receiving our inheritance from Him.

The blood has already made a way for us to enter God's presence. The price for fellowship was already paid. We must simply open up our hearts until we get right into the face of God and see nothing but Him. Let us get into His presence and cry Abba Father. It is our move – He wants us to get close to Him.

Confession of Faith

- Because of the blood of Jesus, I am now part of the family of God. God is my Father (Romans 8:16,17).

- God loves it when I draw near to Him. I choose to seek His face and to hear His voice. As I come close to my Father God, He draws close to me (Psalm 27:4-8).

- In His presence is everything I need (Psalm 16:11).

- I receive my inheritance and take my position in Christ (Colossians 1:12).

- Thank You, Jesus, for paying the price so I can enjoy the presence of my Father God.

By faith in the blood of Jesus we enjoy perfect fellowship with the Father God, and in His presence we have perfect peace that He will perfect what concerns us.

~ Mark Hankins

CHAPTER 11

That's Perfect

So with that one sacrifice He made us holy and brought us into perfect union with God.

~ *Hebrews 10:14 (Laubach)*

For by one sacrifice, valid for ever, he enabled men to enter into perfect communion with God.

~ *Hebrews 10:14 (Barclay)*

The word *perfect* is used thirteen times in the book of Hebrews. Several times it is used in reference to the law and the Old Testament system of sacrifices that were not perfect. The law could not produce a perfect redemption, perfect reconciliation, or a perfect fellowship. Nor could it perfect the conscience of man. It could not reach the root of the problem.

> *It was a perfect sacrifice by a perfect person to perfect some very imperfect people.*

When referring to what God did in Christ, Paul said it was *perfect*. Even the law and the prophets looked on the sacrifice of Jesus and said it was perfect. What Jesus did on the cross produced a perfect righteousness to totally set you free. Now, you are free from sin consciousness, a sense of failure, guilt, or shame, so that you can come before the Father God with perfect fellowship.

Paul refers to God as "Abba Father" or "Daddy God." The Pharisees got upset because they saw God as some austere God that was so far off that they really could not approach Him. But Jesus, through His sacrifice, brought us right into the presence of God. He's our Father God. We can even call Him the most intimate term, "Daddy!"

Perfect Sacrifice

For by one offering he hath perfected for ever them that are sanctified.

~ *Hebrews 10:14*

The Message Bible translates Hebrews 10:14 this way: "It was a perfect sacrifice by a perfect person to perfect some very imperfect people." I like that! Jesus was the "perfect" sacrifice. When God saw the sacrifice of Jesus, He said, "That's Perfect!"

In the Old Covenant, there had to be a perfect sacrificial animal offered to atone for sins and to receive blessings in the covenant. The word *covenant* means "to cut till the blood flows." It is an ancient rite that signifies that "two persons enter into the closest, the most enduring, and the most sacred of compacts, as friends and brothers..." (Clay H. Trumbull).

Forasmuch as ye know that ye were not redeemed with corruptible things, as silver and gold...But with the precious blood of Christ, as of a lamb without blemish and without spot.

~ *1 Peter 1:18,19*

And ye shall offer that day...a he lamb without blemish...

> ~ *Leviticus 23:12*

...He is brought as a lamb to the slaughter...

> ~ *Isaiah 53:7*

When the sacrificial lamb was brought to the priest, it was the lamb that was examined. The worshipper was cleansed and accepted, not based on his own perfection, but on the perfection of the sacrifice.

When we come to God, we don't bring our own goodness, but we can draw near to God based upon the perfection of Jesus, the Lamb, slain from the foundation of the world. God, our Father, invites us to come close and enter into intimate fellowship with Him. Because of His perfect sacrifice, we are perfected.

Perfect Union

But he that is joined unto the Lord is one spirit.

> ~ *1 Corinthians 6:17*

And the glory which thou gavest me I have given them;
that they may be one, even as we are one; I in them, and
thou in me, that they may be made perfect in one...

> ~ *John 17:22,23*

God sees us through the blood of Jesus and accepts us based on the condition of His perfect sacrifice. He made us holy through His blood and brought us into union with God. No longer are we struggling to be good on our own because now we share His life, His nature, and His ability. Now, God has put His laws in our hearts and has written them in our minds (Hebrews 10:16). We shared the death of Christ, and sin has no more dominion over us. We also share in His life and enter into union with Christ. He is the Vine and we are the branches.

> *God sees us through the blood of Jesus and accepts us based on the condition of His perfect sacrifice.*

There are two ordinances in the Church that show clearly the union we share with God through Jesus' blood. They are communion and water baptism. In communion, we drink His blood and eat His flesh spiritually as we take the bread and the cup. His blood and life are applied by faith to show that we have been joined to Him and are part of His body (1 Corinthians 11:24,25).

Water baptism is an external demonstration of the spiritual work of the cross. It shows our death with Jesus to sin, and also our resurrection with Him to new life (Romans 6). It is no longer I who live, but Christ who lives in me! This joy, liberty, and power is ours because the blood of Jesus has brought us into perfect union with God.

Perfect Worship

For the law having a shadow of good things to come, and not the very image of the things, can never with those sacrifices which they offered year by year continually make the comers thereunto perfect...because that the worshippers once purged should have had no more conscience of sins.

~ *Hebrews 10:1,2*

Every year there were sacrifices made for the sins of the people under the Old Covenant. It was a constant reminder of their shortcomings and sins. Most of the church world still lives with sin consciousness because they don't understand all that Jesus' blood has done for them. It is

very difficult to worship God when you're feeling guilty
about what you did or didn't do. That's what religion will
teach, and then leave you feeling hopeless and fearful of
God. Here are some other translations of Hebrews 10:1,2:

*The Jewish law was no more than a shadow of the good
things which are to come; you will not find in it the true
expressions of these realities. By going on making the
same sacrifices which are offered year after year for
ever, the law can never perfect those who are trying to
find a way into God's presence. If these sacrifices could
have done this, they would obviously have ceased to be
offered, because the worshipper would have been once
and for all cleansed, and would no longer be haunted by
the sense of sin.*

~   *Barclay*

*...They would no longer have any guilt or consciousness
of sin.*

~   *Amplified*

*For once you get a congregation genuinely forgiven of
its sins, it no longer has a guilty conscience about them.*

~   *Jordan*

...People whose consciences have been cleansed don't feel guilty any more, and have no further need for sacrifices.

~ Lovett

We can freely worship God when we know our sins have been forgiven and we no longer have a guilty conscience. When we miss the mark and sin, we have an advocate, Jesus our High Priest, who ever lives to pray for us (1 John 2:1). When we confess our sins, He is faithful and just to forgive us and to cleanse us from all unrighteousness (1 John 1:9).

> **We are a worshipping, glorious Church, without spot or wrinkle, washed in the blood of the Lamb.**

The Old Testament law was a shadow of good things to come, but it was not the substance. The Old Testament sacrifices could not do what was necessary to reach the conscience of man and provide perfect fellowship with God. Hebrews 11:1 says, "Now faith is the substance of things hoped for, the evidence of things not seen." The law was a shadow — it wasn't the real thing. Through faith in the blood of Jesus, you can come right into the Holy of Holies — the very presence of God.

> *But ye are come unto Mt. Zion, and unto the city of the living God, the heavenly Jerusalem, and to an innumerable company of angels, to the general assembly and church of the firstborn, which are written in heaven, and to God the Judge of all, and to the spirits of just men made perfect, and to Jesus the mediator of the new covenant, and to the blood of sprinkling, that speaketh better things than that of Abel.*
>
> ~ *Hebrews 12:22-24*

Because of the cleansing, sanctifying, and unifying power of the blood, we can come face to face with God. We can be changed by His glory and endued with His power and authority. This is not a picture, a type, or a figment of our imagination. It is not a man-made idea, but a reality! We are actually in the presence of angels, Jesus, and those who've gone before. We are surrounded by a great cloud of witnesses and it is all because of the blood of Jesus!

We are a worshipping, glorious Church, without spot or wrinkle, washed in the blood of the Lamb. We are the comers or worshippers, and we can go right into the very presence of God to inquire in His temple.

This is the kind of freedom of worship that Jesus was talking about to the woman at the well. She was talking to Him about religion, and He stopped her and began to tell her of a day coming when true worshippers would worship the Father in spirit and in truth (John 4:23). The Amplified Bible calls truth, reality. Jesus was telling her of the day you and I live in. He knew He would take His own blood into the heavenly Holy of Holies and place it on the altar. He was talking about a day when sins' demands were paid for. A new day of hope, when any person could approach the throne of grace to find mercy and grace to help in the time of need. Because of the blood, we can come boldly, enter in and cry, "Abba, Father." This is the place where you can get real answers for real problems.

> ### *No one can get closer to the God than you can.*

In Luke 18, Jesus told a story about two men who prayed: a Pharisee and a tax collector. The Pharisee was self-righteous and prayed based upon his good deeds, while the tax collector struck his breast and said, "God, be merciful to me, a sinner!" Jesus said that the man who appealed to the mercy of God is the one whose prayers were heard (Luke 18:10-15). When we plead the blood of Jesus, we touch the heart of God and His goodness. No one can get closer to God than you can.

Plead the blood of Jesus and with confidence declare the words of this powerful hymn:

> *What can wash away my sin...*
> *What can make me whole again...*
> *This is all my hope and peace...*
> *This is all my righteousness...*
> *Nothing but the blood of Jesus.*

Through perfect fellowship with God we are changed into the same image from glory to glory and brought into His perfect will. Many people only live in the permissive will of God or in the outside perimeters instead of the center of God's will. As we draw near to God, He will perfect all that concerns us.

The Lord will perfect that which concerneth me...

~ ***Psalm 138:8***

Jesus purchased eternal redemption for us with His own blood. Everything was included in that one sacrifice.

Jesus only had to do it once. Once for all time and eternity... once for all problems...once for all mankind...once for all blessings. His work is perfect. He is working in you that which is well-pleasing in His sight. His perfect will for your life will come to pass through faith in His blood. He is well able to get you in the right place, at the right time, with the right people. You will have to give God thanks and say, "That's Perfect!"

Exactly What You Need

When Trina and I first started traveling, I bought a big Foretravel motor home with dark orange and light orange stripes. It was beautiful. I spent all of my money on this motor home — I mean I didn't have anything left! I would make the payments and we would travel to different cities every weekend, preaching.

We were traveling in this beautiful, well-built motor home when I figured out that we had a problem. When I would get to the RV campground, I didn't have any transportation. I would have to unhook the sewer line and electric line, then drive the motor home to church every night. I decided that I needed to get a car to pull behind the motor home. Since I had spent all of my money on the motor home, I thought *How am I going to get a car?*

A few weeks later, we were in Texas at my dad's church when a man offered me a Ford Pinto. I went with him to look at it. It was rusted out, had different color doors, and looked like dogs had been sleeping in the back seat! "It runs pretty good," he said. "You can have it for $300." I said, "I tell you what, you hold it for me because I know I can afford that."

I went home and told Trina, "I think I found us a car. Someone at the church offered me a Ford Pinto for $300. I can afford that." She said, "You are not going to drive that rusty old Pinto behind this beautiful motor home. Why don't we pray?" I said, "Oh, it's come to that. Alright, let's pray."

We prayed to God for a nice car to pull behind our motor home and then went to Arizona for a meeting. The first night we were there, a man walked up to me and said, "The Lord impressed upon me to give you a car." Now, you might be shouting, but my daddy was a preacher and I know the kind of cars people give away. I said, "Before you give me a car, let's go look at it." He said, "It's practically brand new. I haven't even had it for a year. I bought it for my wife and she doesn't want to drive it." So we went to his house to look at this car. When he raised his garage door, there was a white, almost new, Toyota with two orange stripes on it. It perfectly matched my motor home! I said, "That's perfect!"

> *Never bring a knife to a gunfight! We have supernatural weapons that come from God Himself. You cannot fight a spiritual battle with natural weapons.*

When the enemy tries to get you to settle for some old rusty worn out thing, exercise your faith in the blood of Jesus because God has something perfect for you. It will fit you just right! God can give you exactly what you need and you will say, "That's perfect!" The Lord will perfect that which concerns you through faith in His blood!

Passing the Blood Test

Now the God of peace, that brought again from the dead our Lord Jesus, that great shepherd of the sheep, through the blood of the everlasting covenant, Make you perfect in every good work to do his will, working in you that

which is well-pleasing in his sight, through Jesus Christ;
to whom be glory for ever and ever. Amen.

~ *Hebrews 13:20,21*

In order for a doctor to give you a clean bill of health, you have to pass all of the necessary blood tests. It is critical for your physical well-being to have healthy blood. It is the same for your spiritual well-being. Jesus' blood produced a perfect righteousness that enables us to stand before God free from sin consciousness (Hebrews 10:1,2). Jesus passed the blood test for us. In the *1828 Webster's Dictionary*, the word *perfect* is defined as "to finish or complete so as to leave nothing wanting."

By faith in the blood of Jesus we enjoy perfect fellowship with the Father God. In His presence, we have perfect peace that He will perfect what concerns us.

Never Bring a Knife to a Gunfight

And they overcame him by the blood of the Lamb, and
by the word of their testimony; and they loved not their
lives unto the death.

~ *Revelation 12:11*

God has given us supernatural weapons in order to fight our supernatural adversary. With these weapons, we win in every conflict. The Lord said it to me this way: "Never bring a knife to a gunfight!"

We have supernatural weapons that come from God Himself. You cannot fight a spiritual battle with natural weapons. However, with the weapons of God, you can overcome anything that Satan tries to produce in your life.

A few years ago, Trina and I got a Shar Pei dog. Known as Chinese fighting dogs, these dogs are bred to fight. The particular breed we owned had wrinkles in its skin. We found out later that the wrinkles were actually a defense mechanism. In a dog fight, the Shar Pei's enemy will go for its throat. Instead of hurting the Shar Pei, however, the enemy dog just gets a bunch of extra skin in its mouth. Now having the advantage, the Shar Pei turns around and grabs the other dog around the neck, surprising his enemy and winning the fight.

Like these Shar Pei dogs, we are bred to win. God designed every born-again believer to fight and win. When the devil attacks you, he may think he's got you defeated. But you get to just turn around and say, "Ha! Devil, I've got you! God created me a winner, and you are a defeated foe!"

For the weapons of our warfare are not carnal, but mighty through God to the pulling down of strong holds.

~ *2 Corinthians 10:4*

For we wrestle not against flesh and blood, but against principalities, against powers, against the rulers of the darkness of this world, against spiritual wickedness in high places.

~ *Ephesians 6:12*

I like this confession of faith by Grace Ryerson Roos from her book, *The Blood*:

The Blood of Jesus purges me of every defilement of the enemy.
The Blood of Jesus keeps and guards my mind day and night.
The Blood of Jesus prevents deception and aborts every attempt of the enemy to deceive me.
The Blood of Jesus is my divine covering and protection against all the fiery darts of the evil one.
Yea, the Blood of JESUS IS ALIVE! So full of life and grace it perfects that which concerneth me—reconciling everything in me to the perfect will of God every day and in every way.

In the Old Testament, God told the Israelites to place the blood on the doorposts and the destroyer would pass over their homes. Somebody had to get out there and apply the blood. It was not interest in the blood or believing in the blood alone that brought this covering. It was in the application of the blood by faith that brought protection.

The Blood of Jesus Is a Powerful Weapon

The blood of Jesus is a powerful weapon that belongs to every believer. We must apply that blood by faith in every situation. Jesus has done more than enough for our victory. As our faith increases, we access more and more of the benefits of a perfect redemption (Hebrews 9:12). In other words, what Jesus has done for us is perfect, but it is accessed by faith. In 1 Thessalonians 3:10, Paul said that he longed to see the believers in order to perfect that which was lacking in their faith.

Our faith is perfected and strengthened through the ever-increasing light of God's Word. As our faith grows, we receive more and more of our redemption. We are going from "faith to faith." Through faith in the blood of Jesus, we are righteous. We have boldness and we are blessed through faith in His blood (Romans 3:25). Exercise your faith now and apply the blood of Jesus and watch perfection at work in your life. Jesus passed the blood test for you!

Confession of Faith

- Through the blood I have perfect communion with God (Hebrews 1:14).

- I am perfected and sanctified by one offering (Hebrews 10:14).

- Because of the blood of Jesus, I am one spirit with Christ (1 Corinthians 6:17).

- Jesus is in me and I am in Him (John 17:23).

- As I come to worship, there is no more consciousness of sin (Hebrews 10:1,2).

- I am a true worshipper. I worship God in truth or reality (John 4:23).

- Jesus was the perfect sacrifice, and now He perfects that which concerns me (Hebrews 10:14).

- I overcome the enemy by the supernatural weapon of the blood of Jesus and the word of my testimony (Revelation 12:11).

Where the blood of Jesus is honored the Holy Spirit will work. Where the blood flows, the Holy Spirit goes.

~ Mark Hankins

CHAPTER 12

The Holy Spirit and the Blood

For through him we both have access by one Spirit unto the Father.

~ *Ephesians 2:18*

For it is through Him that we have both [whether far off or near] now have an introduction (access) by one [Holy] Spirit to the Father [so that we are able to approach Him].

~ *Ephesians 2:18 (AMP)*

As believers, we have the right of access to the presence of God through the blood of Jesus. But *how* do we get into God's presence? In Ephesians 2:18, Paul gives us the key to unlocking this secret: "For through him we both have access *by one Spirit* unto the Father." The Holy Spirit is essential to accessing the presence of God.

The word *access* not only means "a way in," but also "an introduction." An introduction takes place when someone formally presents two people to each other so they can become acquainted. Because the Holy Spirit knows the Father and lives in you, He introduces you to the Father's presence. He connects you to the Father so you can become more intimately acquainted with Him.

An introduction can also be a formal presentation of royalty. In all royal courts, there is procedure and protocol that must be followed. You wouldn't just go to Buckingham Palace, chase down the queen, and shake her hand! To get into the queen's presence, you would have to follow the proper protocol. The same is true in accessing the presence of God – there is a correct way to enter the throne room, and the Holy Spirit will show you Heaven's procedure and protocol.

The Advocate

And I will ask the Father, and He will give you another Comforter (Counselor, Helper, Intercessor, Advocate,

Strengthener, and Standby), that He may remain with you forever.

~ *John 14:16 (AMP)*

One of the job descriptions of the Holy Spirit is an advocate. P.C. Nelson, a noted linguist and Bible scholar, said three skills are necessary for an advocate to be effective. First, an advocate must have exceptional knowledge. Second, he should have expertise in protocol and procedure. Finally, an advocate must have persuasive speaking ability. In other words, for a person to be a successful advocate, he must know more than the person he represents, he most know the protocol of the court, and he must be an effective communicator.

> ### *The Holy Spirit will show you Heaven's procedure and protocol.*

As an advocate, the Holy Spirit possesses all three skills. Since He is the Spirit of Truth, He knows more than you. He is intimately familiar with the presence of God, and He knows how to communicate truth to you and through you. If you want to go deeper into the presence of God, it is imperative to rely on the Holy Spirit to lead you.

Exceptional Knowledge

But when He, the Spirit of Truth (the Truth-giving Spirit) comes, He will guide you into all the Truth (the whole, full Truth). For He will not speak His own message [on His own authority]; but He will tell whatever He hears [from the Father; He will give the message that has been given to Him], and He will announce and declare to you the things that are to come [that will happen in the future]. He will honor and glorify Me, because he will take of (receive, draw upon) what is Mine and will reveal (declare, disclose, transmit) it to you.

~ *John 16:13,14 (AMP)*

The Holy Spirit will show you how the death, burial, and resurrection of Christ translates into your personal victory.

In referring to the Holy Spirit as the Spirit of Truth, Jesus was ascribing to Him the role of truth-giver. The Holy Spirit was given to show us truth and to help us walk in reality. His job is to take the things of God and transmit them to us. As our advocate, He shows us things to come. He gives us revelation concerning the things of God, His plan for our lives, and our future. He'll even give us revelation as we walk through daily life.

The Holy Spirit will also lead you into the reality of redemption. He will take the types and shadows of redemption and translate them into a living reality for you. He will show you how the death, burial, and resurrection of Christ translate into your personal victory. The Holy Spirit will help you move from theology into reality. He will enlighten you when you read the Word of God, and He'll show you how to apply the Truth to your life. If you listen to Him and His promptings, He will point you to places in the New Covenant and teach you how Jesus' blood has taken care of your redemption.

> *But the Comforter, which is the Holy Ghost, whom the Father will send in my name, he shall teach you all things, and bring all things to your remembrance, whatsoever I have said unto you.*
>
> ~ *John 14:26*

The Holy Spirit will bring the Word of God to your remembrance. He'll even have you singing at the most unusual times. Sometimes a song may just roll out of your spirit, and you'll find yourself singing all day. That's the

Holy Spirit bringing the Word back to your remembrance.

Psalm 32:6,7 in the Amplified says, "...When the great waters [of trial] overflow, they shall not reach [the spirit in] him. You are a hiding place for me; You, Lord, preserve me from trouble, You surround me *with songs and shouts* of deliverance..."

When adversity and trouble are coming against your flesh and mind, the Spirit of God inside you will rise up and have you singing. You'll say, "That was close, devil, but it did not reach my spirit. It didn't get to me because a mighty fortress is our God. There is a hiding place in my spirit. I still have victory, peace, and joy on the inside!" When trials and attacks come, the Holy Spirit will give you a song to sing. In the midnight hour, you'll be singing songs of deliverance inspired by the Holy Spirit!

Expertise in Protocol

Back in the Old Testament, God had set certain procedures in place for the priest to enter the Holy of Holies. Although things have changed under the New Covenant, there is still a right way to enter God's presence. As your advocate, the Holy Spirit will teach you how to access the presence of God, how to reverence His presence, and how to honor the blood.

> ## *Rejoicing is divine protocol demonstrating your faith in the blood of Jesus.*

After the priest made the annual sacrifice, God commanded the Israelites to rejoice for the next seven days. That week was called the "time of our joy" (see Chapter 16 for more details). The sacrifice was made, and the forgiveness had come. Because the Holy Spirit knows the protocol of redemption, He will lead you to rejoice as well. Jesus has already paid the price, and you have been forgiven. The Holy Spirit will prompt you to get happy, sing, and shout about your redemption. Rejoicing is divine protocol demonstrating your faith in the blood of Jesus.

Isaiah 64:5 (NKJV) says, "You meet him who rejoices..." God will meet with you when you start rejoicing about your salvation. The Holy Spirit will teach you how to rejoice. In fact, Romans 14 tells us that the kingdom of God is joy in the Holy Ghost. As you cooperate with the Holy Spirit, He will show you how to celebrate the blood.

Persuasive Speaking Ability

But when the Comforter is come, whom I will send unto you from the Father, even the Spirit of truth, which proceedeth from the Father, he shall testify of me.

~ *John 15:26*

Finally, as your advocate, the Holy Spirit will communicate the truth of God's Word to you and through you. He will help you plead your case. He will lead you into the confession of God's Word.

The Holy Spirit will also teach you how to plead the blood. He'll not only bring scriptures about the blood back to your remembrance, but He will prompt you to plead the blood over your life as well. When the enemy is attacking you, the Holy Spirit will say, "Don't just let the devil beat up on you. Say something!"

If sickness is trying to latch onto you, the Holy Spirit will lead you to speak healing over your body. If you're obeying His promptings, you'll find yourself saying, "By Jesus' stripes I am healed. Jesus has redeemed me from the curse of the law. The blood was shed for me. Thank God, I am the healed of the Lord!" If lack is starting to show up in your life, the Holy Spirit will nudge you to start speaking the Word over your finances. You'll say,

"Lack does not belong to me. Jesus redeemed me from the curse of poverty. All my needs are met. All my bills are paid. I plead the blood over my finances!"

The Holy Spirit is such a wonderful helper to the believer. He'll lead us into the presence of God and show us how to sing and rejoice over our redemption. He'll prompt us to plead the blood and confess the Word. Because He knows all Truth, He will guide us into the reality of our redemption. He is our teacher, our helper, our strengthener, our standby, and our advocate. Thank God we have access into His presence by the blood and with the help of the mighty Holy Spirit.

Confession of Faith

- God has given the Holy Spirit to me as my advocate. Because the Holy Spirit is the Spirit of Truth, He reveals truth to my spirit (John 14:16,17, 26; John 15:26).

- The Holy Spirit shows me how to translate the death and resurrection of Christ into my personal victory (John 16:13,14).

- The Holy Spirit leads me into the presence of the Father. As I listen to Him and obey His promptings, I'll sing, shout, and rejoice over my redemption (Ephesians 2:18).

Pleading the blood is synonymous with faith in the blood. When we plead the blood, we are making a confession of the mercy provided by God through Jesus Christ.

~ Mark Hankins

CHAPTER 13

Win Your Case by Pleading the Blood

I, even I, am he that blotteth out thy transgressions for mine own sake, and will not remember thy sins. Put me in remembrance: let us plead together: declare thou, that thou mayest be justified.

~ *Isaiah 43:25,26*

The word *plead* is a legal term that means "to present a case in a court of law." It also means "a cry for mercy." The voice of the accuser will tell you that you are guilty and condemned. He wants you to think that you will never pass the test and get God's blessing.

The *1828 Webster's Dictionary* defines the word *pleadings* as "the mutual altercations between the plaintiff and defendant, or written statements of the parties in support of their claims, comprehending the declaration, count, or narration of the plaintiff, the plea of the defendant in reply, the replication of the plaintiff to the defendant's plea, the defendant's rejoinder, the plaintiff's sur-rejoinder, the defendant's rebuttal, the plaintiff's sur-rebuttal, etc. until the question is brought to issue, that is, to rest on a single point." A *pleader* is "one that offers reasons for or against; one that attempts to maintain by argument."

> *Your bringing your case to rest on a single point*
> *- His blood alone has done everything.*

Wherefore I will yet plead with you, saith the Lord, and with your children's children will I plead.

~ *Jeremiah 2:9*

O Lord, thou hast pleaded the causes of my soul; thou hast redeemed my life.

~ *Lamentations 3:58*

When we plead the blood, we are making a confession of the mercy provided by God through Jesus Christ. It is a declaration of His righteousness. Your bringing your case to rest on a single point - His blood alone has done everything.

So when you stand in front of life's difficulties, the voice of the accuser will tell you that you are guilty. He may ask, "How do you plead — guilty or not guilty?" Because you have an advocate with the Father, you can boldly say, "I plead the blood!"

...And if any man sin, we have an advocate with the Father, Jesus Christ the righteous: and he is the propitiation for our sins: and not for ours only, but also for the sins of the whole world.

~ 1 John 2:1,2

There must be a continuous application of the blood to your life by faith. When the enemy launches accusations against you, you have to offer a rebuttal! Pleading the blood is synonymous with faith in the blood. You can bring your case to rest because faith in His blood is all that is necessary for your total victory.

Your case rests on what Jesus Christ has done for you in His death, in His burial, and in His resurrection. He is alive! He has won victory for you in every area of your life!

> ### *The blood of Jesus cleanses you from sin in all of its forms and manifestations.*

So put God in remembrance of His promise. Get up every morning and say, "I plead the blood of Jesus over my family, over my mind, over my thoughts, over my past, over my future, and over my conscience! I'll not be guilty. I'll not be condemned. I'll not be accused. Devil, you are not having my children, you're not having my marriage, and you're not having my body. I have won this case! I plead the blood!"

Exercise Faith in the Blood

Through faith in the blood of Jesus you can stop the accuser. You can get in the glory of God and receive God's best blessings. The blood of Jesus cleanses you from sin in all of its forms and manifestations (1 John 1:7). This cleansing is a continual cleansing. He will make you perfect in every good work.

He will get you in the right place, at the right time, with the right people, doing the right thing, fulfilling the will of God! It is not by your own works or struggle, but through faith in the blood!

> *...By the blood (that sealed, ratified) the everlasting agreement (covenant, testament), Strengthen (complete, perfect) and make you what you ought to be and equip you with everything good that you may carry out His will...*
>
> ~   *Hebrews 13:20, 21 (AMP)*

Three things happen when you begin to exercise your faith in the blood. First, you are restored to communion and fellowship with God. You are escorted right into His presence. Second, you can receive the blessing of the Lord. Finally, you can stop the devil and every scheme and attack upon your life because dominion has been restored!

The last condition is exercising faith in the power of the blood. It is not as if we, through our faith, give the blood its effectiveness. No, the blood always retains its power and effectiveness, but our unbelief closes our hearts and hinders its operation. Faith is simply the removal of that hindrance, the setting open of our hearts, for the divine power by which the living Lord will bestow His blood.

~ *Andrew Murray*

Faith cometh by hearing and hearing by the Word of God (Romans 10:17). You have to feed on the Word over and over again. Jesus said in John 6:63, "...the words that I speak unto you, they are spirit, and they are life." When you take the Word concerning the blood and meditate on it, then your spirit literally begins to feed on it. It will get on the inside of you.

My wife, Trina, received the following words of victory from the Lord in prayer. Exercise your faith in the blood by making this confession with boldness and full assurance of faith:

God is on my side,
For the blood has been applied.
Every need shall be supplied,
And nothing shall be denied.
So I enter into rest,
And I know that I am blessed.
I have passed the test,
And I will get God's best!

More Than Conquerors

Who shall separate us from the love of Christ? Shall tribulation, or distress, or persecution, or famine, or nakedness, or peril, or sword?...Nay in all these things we are more than conquerors through him that loved us.

~ *Romans 8:35,37*

Nothing can separate you from the love of God once you understand that in the blood of Jesus is the measure of God's love for you! We are more than conquerors through Him that loved us. Our faith is in His blood. God loved you so much that He produced a righteousness through the blood of Jesus that gives you right standing with Him. You are free from a sense of guilt and shame, and through faith in the blood, you can come boldly right into the presence of God! Now, with confidence, you can boldly confess that this righteousness God has produced in you has made you more than a conqueror through Christ Jesus who loved you and gave Himself for you!

Confession of Faith

- When I plead the blood, I am justified. God blots out my sins and He will not remember them (Isaiah 43:25,26).

- Jesus has pleaded the cause of my soul and redeemed my life (Lamentations 3:58).

- I have an advocate with the Father who is Jesus (1 John 2:1).

- The blood of Jesus cleanses me from sin in all its forms and manifestations (1 John 1:7 AMP).

- Nothing can separate me from the love of Christ (Romans 8:35).

- I am more than a conqueror through Him who loved me (Romans 8:37).

- I win my case because I plead the blood. I plead the blood of Jesus over my family, over my mind, over my past, over my future, and over my conscience.

The blood must have the same place in our hearts that is has with God. From the beginning of God's dealings with man, yes, from before the foundation of the world, the heart of God has rejoiced in that blood. Our hearts will never rest, nor find salvation, until we, too, learn to walk and glory in the power of that blood.

~ Andrew Murray

CHAPTER 14

Application of the Blood

And they shall take of the blood, and strike it on the two side posts and on the upper door post of the houses.... For the Lord will pass through to smite the Egyptians; and when he seeth the blood upon the lintel, and on the two side posts, the Lord will pass over the door, and will not suffer the destroyer to come in unto your houses to smite you.

~   *Exodus 12:7,23*

In Exodus 12, the children of Israel came out of Egypt. God told them, "Place the blood on the doorposts of your home and then stay inside your house. When the destroyer comes over, he'll pass over you because of the blood." So it was by the blood that they were protected from the destroyer. Not only were they protected, but by the blood, they were also delivered from the bondage of Egypt. Psalm 105:37 says, "He brought them forth also with silver and gold: and there was not one feeble person among their tribes." How many of them were there? Over one million. If you include women and children, there may have been three million. So out of approximately three million people, there was not one sick among them. No high blood pressure, no cancer, no runny noses, no arthritis, nobody was limping, nobody had bad eyes, and nobody had bad teeth! Everyone came out strong and healthy!

Benefits of the Blood

Not only were all of the people of Israel healed, but God brought them forth with silver and gold. This simply means that God doesn't just want you to come out of Egypt—Satan's dominion—but He also wants to heal your body and bless your finances. These are the benefits of the blood.

The Bible goes on to say that God gave the Israelites the lands of the heathen. This means they learned something about applying the blood that not only redeemed and delivered them, but also took back everything the devil had stolen from them and more! They were healthy in their bodies *and* had money in their pockets. As you can imagine, this was a happy group of people. The Bible says that God brought them forth with joy!

> *As you begin to understand the benefits of the blood, you will take these scriptures on the blood and exercise your faith.*

When the children of Israel applied the blood, God liked what He saw so much that He rained down "donuts" from Heaven every morning! God brought them out in grand style because of the blood. As you begin to understand the benefits of the blood, you will take these scriptures on the blood and exercise your faith. You will do this not only through knowledge of what the blood has done for you, but by releasing your faith and speaking what the Word has to say about the blood.

Speak and sing about your victory in the blood! Any time you feel like the devil is messing with your body, tormenting your mind, or coming at your family, you ought to find every song you can on the blood of Jesus and sing them all through your house! Find every scripture you can and speak them over and over again because the blood of Jesus will put the devil on the run!

> **In the Old Testament when the blood was shed, the fire of God would fall, the glory of God would be seen, and the voice of God would be heard.**

The Blood Will Get Your Stuff Back

But into the second went the high priest alone once every year, not without blood, which he offered for himself, and for the errors of the people.

~ *Hebrews 9:7*

When you apply the blood of Jesus, not only will it put the devil on the run, but it will also put a stop to the enemy and get your stuff back. If the devil has stolen anything from you, you can say, "Devil, the blood of Jesus is against you. Now my health is springing forth speedily, and my money is coming in to me right now!" In the New Testament believers are called priest. Now Jesus blood is effective and must be used in intercessory prayer as you "stand in the gap" asking God to forgive the sins of others (2 Chronicles 7:14 and 1 John 5:16).

The High Priest would go into the presence of God once a year but not without blood. The blood purchased every aspect of your redemption and salvation. As a matter of fact, the progression in the Old Testament was so simple, that when blood was shed, the fire of God would fall, the glory of God would be seen, and the voice of God would be heard.

The Blood Cleanses Your Conscience

The blood of Jesus has to be applied in two places in order for it to be effective. According to Hebrews 9:12, the blood reached into Heaven and purchased our eternal redemption. However, the blood is not only applied in Heaven but also in our hearts. For the blood of Jesus to be effective in our lives, it has to purge our conscience.

Through faith in the blood, God has also given us the authority to cleanse ourselves. When the blood of Jesus is applied to our conscience, the voices of condemnation, accusation, failure, and guilt are silenced!

> *The blood that availed so powerfully in heaven and over hell is all-powerful in a sinner's heart, too. It is impossible for us to think too highly of, or to expect too much from, the power of Jesus' blood.*
>
> ~ *Andrew Murray*

Now, with confidence, your heart rises up with great expectation, a confession of faith comes out of your mouth! This opens up the supernatural and lets God come marching right into every situation in your life. The blood that reaches both Heaven and your heart cleanses your conscience.

The blood of Jesus has been applied in Heaven and we must apply it to our hearts by faith.

Are You Washed in the Blood?

On the Day of Atonement, 160,000 lambs were killed. When Solomon's Temple was dedicated, there were 400,000 lambs slain. When the blood flowed down from the temple, it flowed into the brook which was called Kidron. The brook ran red with blood not just for a few hours, but for many days. When the people saw this brook running red, it reminded them of the tremendous cost of sin and the price that was paid for them to be made right with God. The stains of sin are cleansed beneath the flow of the blood of Jesus. The blood of Jesus cleanses us from all sin and enables us to meet with God.

I like the words of the following hymns because they serve as a reminder of the tremendous price that Jesus paid for the cleansing of our sins:

> *There is a fountain filled with blood,*
> *drawn from Emmanuel's veins.*
> *And sinners plunged beneath that flood,*
> *lose all their guilty stains.*

Have you been to Jesus for the cleansing power

Are you washed in the blood of the Lamb

Are you fully trusting in His grace this hour

Are you washed in the blood of the Lamb

Are you washed in the blood

In the soul-cleansing blood of the Lamb

Are your garments spotless

Are they white as snow

Are you washed in the blood of the Lamb

His Blood Was the Payment

Hebrews 9:12 says, "Neither by the blood of goats and calves, but by his own blood he entered in once into the holy place, having obtained eternal redemption for us." Jesus obtained eternal redemption for us. The word *redemption* simply means "ransom, deliverance, or freedom through the payment of a price."

For if the blood of bulls and of goats, and the ashes of an heifer sprinkling the unclean, sanctifieth to the purifying of the flesh: How much more shall the blood of Christ, who through the eternal Spirit offered himself without spot to God, purge your conscience from dead works to serve the living God?

~ *Hebrews 9:13,14*

Jesus purchased our release. We were held hostage by the devil, and the blood of Jesus was the payment or ransom for our release. Jesus purchased our eternal freedom from sin and Satan with His blood.

Eternal means *forever*. Other translations say that Jesus purchased our permanent deliverance. The Amplified Bible says that Jesus purchased our "complete redemption and everlasting release." He did not leave anything out. Everything we need—spirit, soul, body, finances, and family—He has provided through His blood.

Sprinkle the Blood

Hebrews 9:19 says that Moses sprinkled both the book and the people with the blood. He had spoken every precept to all the people according to the law. He applied the blood saying, "...This is the blood of the testament which God hath enjoined unto you" (verse 20).

Moses then sprinkled the tabernacle and all of the vessels of the ministry. Hebrews 9:22 says, "And almost all things are by the law purged with blood; and without shedding of blood is no remission."

In the Old Testament, when the people came to meet with God and worship Him, a lot of blood was present. In other words, if they wanted to move into the presence of God, blood had to be sprinkled because it is the highest act of worship. The blood enabled the people to go right into His presence.

The elements and the power of the blood are still the same today. So take the blood of Jesus and sprinkle it over your life. Speak the Word of God in faith over your circumstances. Everything you need has been provided by the blood of Jesus.

Confession of Faith

- Because I apply the blood of Jesus to my home, the Lord will not allow the destroyer to come into my house to destroy my family, my possessions, or me (Exodus 12:23).

- By His own blood, Jesus obtained eternal redemption for me (Hebrews 9:12).

- The blood of Jesus reaches the highest place in Heaven, and it also reaches the deepest place of my heart. The blood of Jesus cleanses me from all sin and enables me to meet with God. Everything I need, He has provided. The blood of Jesus is applied to my conscience, and the voices of condemnation, accusation, failure, and guilt are silenced. With confidence my heart rises up with great expectation! My faith in the blood of Jesus opens up the supernatural and lets God come marching right into every situation in my life.

God is on my side,
For the blood has been applied.
Every need shall be supplied,
And nothing shall be denied.
So I enter into rest,
And I know that I am blessed.
I have passed the test,
And I will get God's best.

~ Trina Hankins

CHAPTER 15

Lift Up Your Voice

And ye shall take a bunch of hyssop, and dip it in the blood that is in the bason, and strike the lintel and the two side posts with the blood that is in the bason; and none of you shall go out at the door of his house until the morning.

~ *Exodus 12:22*

Purge me with hyssop, and I shall be clean: wash me, and I shall be whiter than snow.

~ *Psalm 51:7*

Earlier, we talked about some of the Old Testament types and shadows that represent various aspects of redemption. One of the symbols used in the Old Covenant was a hyssop branch. This branch was used to apply the sacrificial blood during Passover. Before the Israelites left Egypt, the Lord instructed them to take a hyssop branch, dip it into the blood from the lamb they had killed, and apply it to the doorposts of their homes. When the destroyer came during the night, he would pass over the houses where the blood had been applied (Exodus 12).

> *Mere interest or belief in the blood is not enough. The blood must be applied in faith.*

Today, instead of using a hyssop branch to apply the blood, we use our mouths. When we speak the Word of God, we are applying the blood of Jesus to our lives. Every time we lift up our voice in faith, declaring what the blood has done for us and in us, we are taking that hyssop branch and covering ourselves in the blood.

Mere interest or belief in the blood is not enough. The blood must be applied in faith. When you get up in the morning, you need to open your mouth and apply the blood. Start saying, "I plead the blood over my mind, over my faults, over my past. I plead the blood of Jesus over my family, my children, and my grandchildren. I plead the blood over my finances. Christ has redeemed me from the curse of the law. I'll never be broke another day the rest of my life. By Jesus' stripes, I am healed. I don't have to be sick or poor anymore! I don't have to be oppressed anymore!"

Pleading the Blood Over Your Family

...Behold, Satan hath desired to have you, that he may sift you as wheat: But I have prayed for thee, that thy faith fail not: and when thou art converted, strengthen thy brethren.

~ *Luke 22:31,32*

As I had mentioned before, I went through a rebellious time in life during my teenage years. Because my mom understood the power of faith in the blood, she would always plead the blood over me. I can recall numerous times when I heard Mom say, "I plead the blood of Jesus."

During the time I was backslidden, I was involved in a terrible car accident. I had totaled six cars and thought

I was going to die. By the mercy of God, I survived and came home to find my mom sitting in a rocking chair saying, "I plead the blood. The devil's not going to have you. I plead the blood of Jesus over you." I knew her prayers had saved my life.

All through my rebellious period Mom consistently pleaded the blood over me. No matter what trouble I got into, whether it was a sassy girlfriend or time in jail, Mom would open her mouth and apply the blood of Jesus over my life. One mom can stop the devil in his tracks. The devil would have liked to have had me, but he couldn't because someone was pleading the blood.

We can apply the blood over our home just like the Israelites did in the Old Testament. In Exodus chapter 12, Moses instructed every family to take the blood of a lamb and apply it over the door of their house. Jesus is the Lamb for every household to gain protection against all the power of darkness. You can declare, "All my children are taught of the Lord and great is their peace. I am established in peace and far from oppression. No weapon formed against me shall prosper" (Isaiah 54:13,14,17).

When you plead the blood of Jesus, you can have confidence like the woman in Proverbs 31:21(AMP): "She fears not the snow for her family, for all her household are doubly clothed in scarlet." This verse has reference to Rahab the harlot, who hid Joshua and Caleb as they spied out the city of Jericho. They gave her a promise in Joshua 2:18-21 that all her family and possessions would be preserved from judgment if they were in her house when the city was taken. The sign she was given was a scarlet cord she hung out her window, the sign of the blood covenant. When the walls fell, her entire family was safe because she had faith in the power of the blood.

One mom can stop the devil in his tracks!

If we plead the blood of Jesus over our homes, our family members and possessions will stand in time of judgment and difficulty while the rest of society crumbles. The Bible tells us that no weapon formed against us shall prosper. With the blood as our covering, our homes and families will be preserved during the days of evil.

Perhaps some of you have family members who are not serving God. Don't let the devil have his way in their lives. Take the hyssop branch of your mouth, lift up your voice in faith, and apply the blood of Jesus over them. Start saying, "I plead the blood of Jesus over my family. I plead the blood over my children. Satan cannot have them. As for me and my house, we will serve the Lord."

Freedom to Speak Up

Having therefore, brethren, boldness to enter into the holiest by the blood of Jesus.

~ *Hebrews 10:19*

Therefore, brethren, since we have full freedom and confidence to enter into the [Holy of] Holies [by the power and virtue] in the blood of Jesus.

~ *Hebrews 10:19 (AMP)*

Hebrews 10:19 tells us that we can boldly enter the Holy of Holies because of the blood. One translation of that verse says we have "freedom of speech" in the Holy Place. In other words, our entrance into the presence of God comes through freedom of speech or words of faith.

Faith is always expressed by speaking. Whenever we come into the presence of God, we are given freedom to speak words of faith, based on what God said in His

Word. As we apply the blood over our lives, we speak words of faith. We don't have to cower in fear or shame in approaching the throne of God. We can come boldly into the Father's presence, knowing that the blood has given us confidence to speak up in faith.

You Have the Last Word

Do you remember the story of David and Goliath (1 Samuel 17)? The Philistine Goliath had stood before the Israelites, daring someone to fight him. Everyone was too afraid to go against him, for Goliath was a fierce giant. But then came this little shepherd guy named David. Refusing to wear the king's armor, he stepped out into battle with just a slingshot and a few pebbles.

> *Never let the devil have the last word in anything that's going on in your life.*

Goliath began to taunt David, saying, "Am I a dog, that you should come against me with sticks?" Boldly, David answered, "You come to me with a sword and a spear, but I come to you in the name of the Lord of hosts. This day, the Lord will deliver you into my hand." And with those words of confidence, David put a pebble in his slingshot, aimed for his enemy, and slung the stone right into the giant's forehead.

> **The Word of God is a spoken thing. It was spoken before it was written, and it was written so it could be spoken.**

Before David even launched his weapon, he ran at Goliath with his words. He spoke to his enemy, declaring his covenant with God and his full victory. Although Goliath stood tall before him, shouting and mocking, David talked back. There was a war of words going on there. But David had been out in the fields, worshipping God. His boldness came from knowing his God and his covenant. The moment the enemy spoke words of defeat and fear, David fought back with words of courage and victory.

Anytime the devil comes at you with lies of failure, sickness, lack or death, you just start talking back to him.

Never let him have the last word in anything that's going on in your life. If he starts talking to you, just say, "I'm not done talking yet." Before you can win the fight of faith, you must win the war of words. As you have heard me say before, never run at your giant with mouth shut. The devil might talk to you many times with words of defeat, but each time, open your mouth and talk back to him with the Word. You can say, "Hey, devil, I got something else for you here. Jesus said He'll never leave me or forsake me. I can boldly say the Lord is my helper, and I will not fear what man shall do unto me." Let the Word of God spoken through you be the last word in any situation.

There's Power in Your Mouth

The Word of God is a spoken thing. It was spoken before it was written, and it was written so it could be spoken. The Bible says that man shall not live by bread alone, but by every word that proceeds out of the mouth of God. The Word didn't come from just ink. The Word came out of the mouth of God. It came out of God Himself.

Every word in the Bible is full of power. The devil is scared every time you just open your Bible to read. The

Word of God is full of faith, and when you begin to speak it, your mouth becomes loaded with power!

If you study the Bible, you will notice that anytime God wanted to change someone's life, He always touched that person's mouth. When God took a coal and placed it on Isaiah's mouth, iniquity was taken from him. After his mouth was set on fire, Isaiah said, "Here am I, send me!"

The prophet Jeremiah complained he was not up to the task God had given him because he was just a child. But God touched his mouth and said, "I'm putting My words in your mouth, and when you speak, it's going to uproot and plant some things. When you speak, a few things will be torn down, while others will be built up."

There may be some things in your life, in your mind, or in your imagination that have been built up over the years. Perhaps the enemy has even told you those things will stay in your life forever and never come down. But the moment you take the Word of God and start speaking to your mind, to your body, and to your circumstances, a demolition crew has just entered the picture. The Word of God spoken through you will tear down those things the devil has said will always be there. The depression or poverty that has plagued you for so long will start coming down as you begin speaking the Word. No matter what the devil has spoken to you, you can just say, "No. That can't stay that way anymore. I'm changing the scenery around here. I'm going to tear that thing down with the Word in my mouth!"

> **Before you can win the fight of faith, you must win the war words.**

Have you ever watched a show on television where a demolition crew comes in and blows up old buildings? Some of those buildings took years to build and are dozens of stories high. Although those structures seem to be indestructible, once the explosives are placed in strategic points and set off, the buildings come down in ten seconds' time. Bam! It's amazing to watch.

Now, if man can tear down a skyscraper with dynamite, how much more can God tear down the strongholds in your life? He is saying to you, "I'm going to strategically place a few dynamite charges in some areas of your soul where the devil's been tormenting you. I'll bring that thing down in the next ten seconds and change the scenery in your life."

With the Word of God in our mouths, things are coming down! Thoughts, imaginations, and reasonings are coming down. Identities are being changed by the power of the Word of God. We're taking that hyssop branch of faith and applying the blood to our lives. The destroyer cannot come in because of the blood. Our families are saved because of the blood. Our souls are restored because of the blood. As we lift up our voices in faith, speaking the Word and declaring our covenant, the enemy doesn't stand a chance. We win by the blood!

Confession of Faith

- I have boldness and confidence to enter the Holy of Holies because of the blood of Jesus (Hebrews 10:19).

- I have freedom of speech in the presence of God (Hebrews 10:19).

- I plead the blood of Jesus over my mind and over my body. I plead the blood of Jesus over my family, my marriage, and my children.

- No weapon formed against me or my family shall prosper (Isaiah 54:17).

There must be a "full assurance of faith" that there is a Holy Place where we can dwell and walk with God; that the power of the precious blood has conquered sin so perfectly that nothing can prevent our undisturbed fellowship with God; that the way that Jesus has sanctified through His flesh is a living way, which carries those who tread on it with eternal living power; that the great "high priest over the house of God" can "save them to the uttermost that come unto God by him" (Hebrews 7:25); and that He by His Spirit, works in us everything that is necessary for life in the Holiest. These things we must believe and hold fast in the "full assurance of faith."

~ Andrew Murray

CHAPTER 16

A New System of Worship

For the law having a shadow of good things to come, and not the very image of the things, can never with those sacrifices which they offered year by year continually make the comers thereunto perfect.

~ *Hebrews 10:1*

Under the Old Covenant, the people had to offer a sacrifice every year when they came to worship. Their sacrifice was to be a perfect, flawless lamb without blemish or spot. The priest examined the sacrifice, if the sacrifice was perfect the worshipper was accepted based on the condition of the sacrifice. In other words, the priest wasn't examing the worshipper, he was examing the sacrifice.

When Jesus offered Himself for our sins on the cross, He became the perfect sacrifice accepted by God. Now, as we come to worship the Father through the blood, He accepts our worship, not based on our condition, but on the perfect sacrifice of His Son.

This perfect blood sacrifice of Jesus forever changed the system of worship. No longer are yearly sacrifices needed to cover the sins of people. The blood of Jesus, offered one time only, abolished the sin problem. Those who believe on His sacrifice are now accepted into the presence of God to fellowship, to commune, and to worship.

> *But ye are come into mount Zion, and unto the city of the living God, the heavenly Jerusalem, and to an innumerable company of angels, To the general assembly and church of the firstborn, which are written in heaven, and to God the Judge of all, and to the spirits of just men made perfect, And to Jesus, the mediator of the new covenant, and to the blood of sprinkling, that speaketh better things than that of Abel.*
>
> ~   *Hebrews 12:22-24*

Notice Hebrews 12 says "Now you are come..." The blood of Jesus has made the way for you to come now into the presence of God. You don't have to wait until you're "good enough" or until you die to have some heaven in your life. The blood of Jesus has made a way for you to come and enjoy fellowship with the Father today. Because of the blood, you now have access into the presence of God.

> *Moving from the types and shadows and move into the reality of His presence.*

As a believer, you are called by God to live in two worlds. You are walking down here on earth in a natural body, but your spirit is hooked up to Heaven. Because your spirit is alive unto God, you can walk and talk with Him at any given moment during the day. Your worship is not based on performance or acts of worthiness, but on the perfect sacrifice of Jesus, the Lamb of God. Through the blood, you can come into that beautiful place of worship with Almighty God. No longer are you living in the type and shadow of the old system of worship. Because of the blood of Jesus, you have come into reality.

Worship in Spirit and Truth

In John chapter four, Jesus encounters a woman at the well and begins to tell her of the living water that comes through Him. Jesus says to her, "Whosoever drinketh of the water that I shall give him shall never thirst; but the water that I shall give him shall be in him a well of water springing up into everlasting life" (verse 14). He then speaks to her of true worship that comes through redemption: "But the hour cometh, and now is, when the true worshippers shall worship the Father in spirit and in truth: for the Father seeketh such to worship him. God is a Spirit: and they that worship him must worship him in spirit and in truth" (verses 23 and 24).

> *Jesus was ushering in a whole new worship system through His blood.*

Jesus was telling the woman that true worshippers no longer have to go to a certain place to worship, as was the Jewish custom. Through His sacrifice, those who seek to worship God can worship Him in spirit and in truth.

The type and shadow of worship has been done away with, and the reality of God's presence has come. Jesus was ushering in a whole new worship system through His blood.

Come and Drink

And the Spirit and the bride say, Come. And let him that heareth say, Come. And let him that is athirst come. And whosoever will, let him take the water of life freely.

~ *Revelation 22:17*

Jesus was telling this woman to come and drink of the water that He offers. To drink means to believe, receive, respond, experience. When you come into the presence of God, you receive with your heart, respond to His Spirit, and experience His power. You don't drink by thinking; you drink by acting and responding. Drinking of this well requires you to receive by faith. It is an act of your spirit.

You can't drink with your mouth closed either. When you drink of the heavenly fountain, you open your mouth wide and receive of the Spirit of God. Something begins to bubble up in your spirit, and you give expression to that with your mouth.

Flowing from the throne of God, this water is full of life. Everything of God is in the water. If you drink of it with your spirit, you will be satisfied. The living water of God offers you healing, joy, peace, and restoration. If you need something from God, come take a drink!

The blood has perfected the system of worship, bringing us into a new and better way. We can now come into the reality of true worship, accessing the presence of God freely. Alive and constant, the water Jesus offers fills us with God Himself, leaving our spirits satisfied. Let us come to that well and drink, drink, drink!

Confession of Faith

- I can come boldly into the presence of God because of the blood of Jesus.

- God accepts my worship, not based on my good works, but on the perfect sacrifice of His Son (Hebrews 10:1).

- I freely drink of the living waters that come from God. I receive healing, joy, peace, and restoration.

- I am coming to Jesus, the mediator of the new covenant, and to the blood of sprinkling, that speaks better things (Hebrews 12:22-24).

- God is a spirit and I worship Him in spirit and in truth (John 4:24).

It is not only the penitent sinner, longing for pardon, who must thus value it. No! The redeemed will see that just as God in His temple sits upon a throne of grace, where the blood is ever in evidence, so there is nothing that draws our hearts nearer to God, filling them with God's love, joy, and glory, as living in a constant, spiritual view of that blood.

~ Andrew Murray

CHAPTER 17

Honor the Blood

Let the world, O Lord be filled with the knowledge of Thee and Thy Son, Jesus Christ. Wash away my sins in the immaculate blood of the Lamb and purge my heart by the Holy Spirit. Daily frame me more and more in the likeness of thy Son.

~ ***George Washington***
First President of the United States

George Washington, the first President of the United States and the father of our country, understood the immense impact of the blood of Jesus. Without it, man's redemption could not have taken place. Only the blood holds the power to wash away every guilty stain of sin and to make us pure and holy. Throughout time, the magnitude of the blood has not diminished. Its transforming and cleansing power is still available for humanity today.

> ***The moment a person is cleansed, the Holy Spirit will fall.***
>
> *- Smith Wigglesworth*

As redeemed children of God, we need to honor the sacrifice made for us in the blood of Jesus. As Heaven's most valuable commodity, it was poured out to satisfy the demands of redemption. Because of the blood, we are free. Precious and powerful, the blood of Jesus deserves to be reverenced and honored.

One way we honor the blood of Jesus is by speaking and singing in faith. Today, like never before, we must apply the blood of Jesus by faith. As we lift up our voices, the realm of both the seen and the unseen powerfully change. Miracles happen when we speak or sing of the blood's power.

Blood Songs and Revival

...Be filled with the Spirit; Speaking to yourselves in Psalm and hymns and spiritual songs, singing and making melody in your heart to the Lord.

~ Ephesians 5:18,19

For He says, I will declare Your [the Father's] name to My brethren; in the midst of the [worshipping] congregation I will sing hymns of praise to You.

~ Hebrews 2:12 (AMP)

Thou art my hiding place; thou shalt preserve me from trouble; thou shalt compass me about with songs of deliverance...

~ Psalm 32:7

The above scriptures point out the importance of singing songs of praise and worship to the Lord. Singing is one way to release our faith in God's goodness, faithfulness, and provision. When we sing songs that focus on the blood, we are encouraged and uplifted in our faith in the blood.

Many of the old hymns carry the redemption doctrine of the blood of Jesus. As a young person in church, I grew up singing numerous "blood songs" that have been passed down from earlier generations. Most of these great hymns on the blood were written during the late 1800's through the early 1900's and preceded some of the greatest outpourings of the Holy Spirit of that era, including the Azusa Street Revival.

The Church must never stop singing about the blood. Even if you don't know the melody, you can speak the words of these hymns by faith. Lyrics such as "This is all my hope and peace" and "This is all my righteousness, nothing but the blood of Jesus" are great confessions of faith of what the blood has done and will continue to do in your life.

Singing redemption songs in faith will open Heaven and your heart to all God has for you. Be encouraged as you lift up your voice because there is great victory when you speak or sing these songs by faith. The blood of Jesus will never lose its power!

When I See Your Blood
by Trina Hankins

When I see Your blood, I know how much You love me
When I apply Your blood, my blinded eyes can see
When I speak Your blood, there's not one thing in me the
   blood cannot cleanse
My heart, my soul, my mind, I surrender to the power of
   Your blood

There's not one thing in me, one thing in me, one thing in
    me that the blood can't cleanse

There's not one thing in me, one thing in me, one thing in
    me that the blood can't cleanse

The Holy Spirit Goes Where the Blood Flows

*But into the second went the high priest alone once every
year, not without blood, which he offered for himself,
and for the errors of the people: The Holy Ghost this
signifying, that the way into the holiest of all was not
yet made manifest...*

              ~ *Hebrews 9:7,8*

*Neither by the blood of goats and calves, but by his
own blood he entered in once into the holy place, having
obtained eternal redemption for us.*

              ~ *Hebrews 9:12*

Scripture shows us how the blood of Jesus and the
Holy Spirit work together. John 7:39 tells us that the Holy
Spirit could not be given until Jesus was glorified. We
find out in Hebrews 9:12 that after Jesus was raised from
the dead, He took His blood into the Holy of Holies once
and for all. It wasn't until Jesus took His own blood and
applied it in Heaven that the Holy Spirit could be poured
out on mankind.

When we honor the blood, we give the Holy Spirit freedom to move. Smith Wigglesworth once said, "The moment a person is cleansed, the Holy Spirit will fall." In other words, when the blood is applied, the Holy Spirit has freedom to work. The instant the blood of Jesus is applied by faith or honored appropriately, the Holy Spirit will change the very atmosphere of our lives.

> *When we honor the blood, we give the Holy Spirit freedom to move.*

In the book of Acts, when Paul and Silas were bound in prison, they prayed and sang praises to God. As they did this all the doors were open, everyone free, and a revival broke out. When we sing in faith about the blood, we create an environment for the Holy Spirit to move among us, both individually and corporately. Whenever we speak words of faith about the blood, we give the Holy Spirit freedom to work. Honoring the blood of Jesus opens the door to the supernatural, allowing the Spirit of God to flow in us and through us. We can expect a move of the Holy Spirit as we honor the blood.

Confession of Faith

- I honor the blood of Jesus and give the Holy Spirit freedom to move.

- Jesus purchased my eternal freedom and my everlasting release when He took His blood into the Holy Place (Hebrews 9:12).

- As I sing about the blood and speak of the blood, I expect the Holy Spirit to move in my life.

- I am filled with the Spirit, speaking to myself in psalms, hymns and spiritual songs, singing and making melody in my heart to the Lord (Ephesians 5:18-19).

- God is my hiding place; He shall preserve me from trouble; he shall compass me about with songs of deliverance (Psalm 32:7)

- When I honor the blood by singing and worshipping God,, Jesus Himself sings hymns of praise to God (Hebrews 2:12).

THE BLOOD
POWER TO
REJOICE

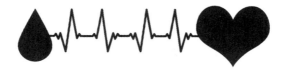

LET US HOLD FAST THE PROFESSION OF OUR
FAITH WITHOUT WAVERING; (FOR HE IS
FAITHFUL THAT PROMISED;)
~ HEBREWS 10:23

BUT LET THE RIGHTEOUS BE GLAD; LET THEM
REJOICE BEFORE GOD: YEA, LET THEM
EXCEEDINGLY REJOICE. SING UNTO GOD, SING
PRAISES TO HIS NAME: EXTOL HIM THAT
RIDETH UPON THE HEAVENS BY HIS NAME JAH,
AND REJOICE BEFORE HIM.
~ PSALM 68:3-4

If you only knew what happens in the spirit when you rejoice, you would rejoice every day!

~ Mark Hankins

CHAPTER 18

The Time of Our Joy

Under the Old Covenant there were certain procedures to follow on the Day of Atonement. God had set specific guidelines for the priests to follow when they entered the Holy of Holies. One of the sacrifices made on the Day of Atonement involved two goats. The first goat was sacrificed in the temple, and its blood was applied to the Mercy Seat. The other goat, the scapegoat, was led into the wilderness and was sacrificed there. The following are excerpts from the book *The Holy Temple of Jerusalem* by Chaim Richman. I like how this book describes what happened on the Day of Atonement and the celebration (the time of joy) that followed.

The high priest then tied a length of crimson-dyed wool between the horns of the scapegoat and tied a similar length of wool around the neck of the goat that was to be sacrificed. The wool was dyed crimson in accordance with the verse, "... though your sins be as scarlet, they shall be as white as snow; though they be red like crimson, they shall be as wool" (Isaiah 1:18).

Arriving at the cliff, the priest removed the crimson wool that the high priest had tied to the scapegoat's horns. He divided it into two pieces, tying one to the animal's horns and the second to a rock so that he would be able to see when the crimson color had turned white and know that atonement had been made for Israel's sins. Then he pushed the goat backward with his two hands.

After he had accomplished his task, the priest who had led the scapegoat walked back to the last booth, and waited there until dark before he returned to Jerusalem – for he had only been permitted to travel this distance in order to fulfill the duty of the scapegoat. After having given the scapegoat to his colleague, the High Priest had to wait until he received word that the scapegoat had reached the desert, and thus he could proceed to the next stage of the day's service. In addition to the crimson wool on the Sanctuary miraculously turning white, this information reached the temple another way. Scouts were positioned at high points all along the route to the cliff and, as the goat was led from one station to the next, these scouts would signal to each other by waving cloths, and when the scapegoat had finally been cast off, the news was relayed back to the temple through the scouts' signal.

Just as the children of Israel rejoiced over the blood, we can rejoice when we understand what the blood has done for us. Years ago, in old-time spirit-filled gatherings, people would be filled with joy and the Holy Ghost. They would take out their handkerchiefs and begin to wave them, signaling that they had the victory. This was a demonstration of joy and celebration.

When the Gospel is preached today, you can look at the faces and the response of those who hear the message and tell who truly believes. Those who understand will respond with joy and praise, dancing, and thanksgiving. Thank God, the blood has been applied through the cross. Our sins have been blotted out once and for all. We are the redeemed children of God. As the scouts signaled to each other, let us signal to one another, telling the glorious message that though our sins were as scarlet, they are now as white as snow; though they were red like crimson, they are now as wool (Isaiah 1:18).

Commanded to Rejoice

After the sacrifice had been accepted, it was time for the Festival of Tabernacle, which was also known as "the time of our joy." The rejoicing took place mainly in the Holy Temple, the central point of Jewish worship.

And ye shall take you on the first day the boughs of goodly trees, branches of palm trees, and the boughs of thick trees, and willows of the brook; and ye shall rejoice before the Lord your God seven days. And ye shall keep it a feast unto the Lord seven days in the year. It shall be a statute forever in your generations: ye shall celebrate it in the seventh month. Ye shall dwell in booths seven days; all that are Israelites born shall dwell in booths. That your generations may know that I made the children of Israel to dwell in booths, when I brought them out of the land of Egypt: I am the Lord your God.

~ *Leviticus 23:40-43*

After the sacrifice had been accepted, the children of Israel were *commanded* to rejoice for seven days. Even the smartest and most influential men in that generation rejoiced and celebrated because they understood what the blood had done.

At the foot of Mount Moriah, in the City of David, there is a natural spring called Siloam, the source of Jerusalem's water. As it is located literally in the shadow of the Holy Temple, it has always had spiritual significance for Israel.

Each day of the festival, the priest went down to Siloam Temple. There, they filled a golden flask with three lug (about ½ liter) of the pure water and returned to the Temple through the West Gate, on the southern side of the court. As they entered the gate, their steps were greeted by the sound of trumpets and shofar blasts, in fulfillment of the prophet's words, "Therefore with joy shall ye draw water out of the wells of salvation" (Isaiah 12:3).

The actual participants in the celebration were not the common folk, but the greatest scholars and the most pious men of the generation – the heads of the Sanhedrin, the sages, the academy heads, and the elders. In the presence of all those assembled in the Holy Temple, these exceedingly righteous men would dance, sing, and rejoice.

These exceedingly righteous men had knowledge and understanding of the blood sacrifices and wine libations together. They had reason to rejoice because they knew these celebrations signified the fulfilling of Isaiah 12:3, which is a type of salvation we receive through Jesus Christ. They were commanded to rejoice because their sins were covered for one year.

> *Rejoice because the blood has been shed and the enemy has been defeated for you.*

Under the New Covenant, we must rejoice because our sins have been remitted eternally when we believe and receive what Jesus has done for us in redemption. We are now made the very righteousness of God! Now we are the temple of the Holy Spirit! Rejoice because the blood has been shed and the enemy has been defeated for you. When anyone believes, there is now a spring of living water flowing, bubbling continually within you (John 4:14). It is what Jesus spoke of to the woman at the well, and it is a time when any believer anywhere may worship the Father in spirit and in truth.

> *But let the righteous be glad; let them rejoice before God: yea, let them exceedingly rejoice.*
>
> ~   *Psalm 68:3*

> *And now shall my head be lifted up above my enemies round about me: therefore will I offer in his tabernacle sacrifices of joy; I will sing, yea, I will sing praises unto the Lord.*
>
> ~   *Psalm 27:6*

Those truly reverent people will break forth into excessive, exceeding, great joy! Philippians 4:4 instructs us to "Rejoice in the Lord always: and again I say, Rejoice." Romans 14:17 tells us "The kingdom of God is righteousness, peace and joy in the Holy Ghost." First Peter 1:8 says, "Whom ye have not seen, you love; in whom, though you see Him not, yet believing, you rejoice with joy unspeakable and full of glory." Heaven's joy is full of glory!

> ## *The glory of God will fill you as you begin to sing, dance, and rejoice!*

When David was a new king, he desired to bring the Ark of the Covenant back to Jerusalem. His first attempt was met with disappointment because the ark wasn't carried on the priest's shoulders and accompanied with joy. He left it in the house of Obed-edom and God's blessing began to come on his household. In 2 Samuel 6 we read how David went again to get the ark. This time he brought back the Ark of the Covenant to Jerusalem with much joy, dancing, and sacrifices. Every six paces, David stopped to offer a blood sacrifice. The glory of the Lord began to fall on them until David danced with all his might and all the house of Israel brought up the ark with shouting, and with the sound of the trumpet. That happened in the Old Covenant.

Now in the New Testament your body is the temple of the Holy Ghost because of the blood of Jesus. The glory of God will fill you as you begin to sing, dance, and rejoice! We have left the type and the shadow and are now living in the reality of righteousness and the very presence of God within. Faith in what God has done demands a response. It is a proper response of "exceedingly righteous" people to rejoice!

A Merry Heart

The joy of the Lord is your strength. With joy you shall draw water from the wells of salvation (Isaiah 12:3) .You can receive healing and every need met as you draw up salvation from the well on the inside with joy! The Word of God is health to all your flesh and a merry heart does good, like a medicine (Proverbs 4:22; 17:22).

> *When you believe and rejoice, the Holy Spirit will take the triumph of Christ and make it real to you.*

We are living in a time when people are depending more and more on pharmaceutical drugs for every physical or mental ache and pain. God has already made provision for our health by His wounds and shed blood on the cross.

When you are facing a physical battle, don't rely on natural medication only — take hold of the power of God as well. Rejoice in the Lord, laugh, and dance. The glory of God will give you strength, hope and healing.

You can put your faith in the blood of Jesus, believe, and then rejoice because healing, deliverance and financial blessing have already been provided. As you release your faith and rejoice, the Holy Spirit will take the triumph of Christ and make it real to you. You will then experience the power of the Living Water from Heaven. Joy is a fruit of the spirit and every fruit will crucify your flesh. You may not feel like it, but as you make the choice to rejoice you'll experience and enjoy all that Jesus' blood purchased for you.

Let us be like the truly righteous men of old. We have left the type and the shadow to live in the reality of true worship. The Bible tells us that God sits in the heavens and laughs (Psalm 2:4). If He is laughing, we should rejoice with Him!

There was a sign on the office desk of a very successful businessman that read, "You have ten seconds to get enthusiastic or get out of my office!" When you believe the Gospel, there is such a joy that nothing in this world can bring. The very presence of the Holy Spirit, the water, and the wine from Heaven is poured into your heart. As they were commanded to rejoice for a week in the Old Covenant, we who have received the Living Water and the wine of the Holy Spirit must respond appropriately with expressions of heavenly, triumphant joy! Let us rejoice and celebrate our victory in the blood of Jesus!

Confession of Faith

- Though my sins were as scarlet, they are now white as snow (Isaiah 1:18).
- I am drinking the water from Jesus and it is springing up like a well in my heart (John 4:14).
- With joy I am drawing up water from the wells of salvation (Isaiah 26:3).
- The joy of the Lord is my strength (Nehemiah 8:10).
- A merry heart does good like a medicine (Proverbs 17:22).

It will become clear that there is no single scriptural idea, from Genesis to Revelation, more constantly and more prominently kept in view than that expressed by the words "the blood."

~ Andrew Murray

CHAPTER 19

Slap That Chicken

And ye shall know the truth, and the truth shall make you free. If the Son therefore shall make you free, ye shall be free indeed.

~ *John 8:32,36*

As a young man, a friend of mine had a job working with chickens. To transport the chickens, they placed them in cages and tied their feet together with strings. When they reached their destination after miles and miles of travel, he would open the cages and cut the strings in order to let the chickens out. But even after they were set free, the chickens would just lay there. They thought they were still bound and refused to get up. My friend had to slap the chickens around a little to get them up and moving. Once they realized they were free, the chickens really enjoyed their freedom. You can imagine the sight of happy chickens running around everywhere!

To this day, many Christians are still lying there, waiting for something to happen so that they can be free. The truth is, you are free! Jesus has already purchased your freedom! Through faith in His blood right now, shake yourself, get up, get moving, and go forward!

The Good News

For I am not ashamed of the gospel of Christ: for it is the power of God unto salvation to every one that believeth; to the Jew first, and also to the Greek. For therein is the righteousness of God revealed from faith to faith: as it is written, The just shall live by faith.

~ Romans 1:16,17

What is the Gospel? The Gospel is the death, burial, and resurrection of Jesus Christ. The central theme of the ten sermons in the book of Acts is the Gospel. Paul's epistles also record what happened in the death, burial, and resurrection of Jesus, not only in what was seen, but in what was unseen. Paul not only records what man saw, but also what God saw. Everything Jesus did, He did it for us. It is set to the credit of our account as though we did it. In the mind of God and in the economy of God, everything Jesus did, He did it for us.

> *When you understand what Jesus did for you, it will make you glad! The good news is not that God can help you, wants to help you, or is someday going to help you, but that He has already helped you!*

The Gospel is good news — a message that makes you glad. It is a celebration of the triumph of Christ. First John 3:8 says, "...For this purpose the Son of God was manifested, that he might destroy the works of the devil." Jesus came to destroy — loosen, undo, dissolve, or unravel — every strategy and scheme of the devil!

When you understand what Jesus did for you, it will make you glad! The good news is not that God can help you, wants to help you, or is someday going to help you, but that He has already helped you!

Resurrection Realities

I am he that liveth, and was dead; and, behold, I am alive for evermore, Amen; and have the keys of hell and of death.

> ~ *Revelation 1:18*

We need to live every day in the light that Jesus is alive. When Jesus was raised from the dead, He took His blood into the heavenly Holy of Holies and obtained eternal redemption for us. Through faith in the blood of Jesus you and I can meet with God. When you meet with God, He will bring radical change to your life.

Who is redemption available to? Romans 3:22 says, "... upon all them that believe, for there is no difference." It is available to everyone who will believe and exercise faith in the blood of Jesus. In other words, our confidence and assurance is in what Jesus did on the cross. His blood was shed to restore our fellowship with God. We can know Him personally and intimately. We can fellowship with Him and receive from Him.

Being justified freely by his grace through the redemption that is in Christ Jesus...through faith in his blood...

> ~ *Romans 3:24,25*

Notice the words and phrases used in these verses: *redemption, in Christ Jesus,* and *through faith in His blood.* Redemption simply means "the purchase of freedom." Jesus purchased our freedom with His own blood. We have faith in His blood because we understand the value and the power in it!

> *Neither by the blood of goats and calves, but by His own blood he entered in once into the holy place, having obtained eternal redemption for us.*
>
> ~ *Hebrews 9:12*

The freedom and redemption that is ours in Christ is not temporary. The Goodspeed translation of Hebrews 9:12 says that His blood "secured our permanent deliverance." It is permanent! It is eternal! Christ hath redeemed us!

> *For the enjoyment of this blessedness, nothing is necessary except faith in the blood. The blood alone has done everything.*
>
> ~ *Andrew Murray*

Our freedom from the curse of the law has already been purchased (Galatians 3:13). In Him we have redemption through His blood (Colossians 1:14). Freedom from the power of sin, Satan, fear, sickness, and poverty is ours today through faith in His blood!

No Special Problems

Jesus paid a very high price for your freedom. Do you think that when you go to God with a problem He says, "Oh, my! I've never seen a problem like this before. I am not going to promise you anything but We'll see what We can do." Then He calls Jesus over, and Jesus says, "Oh, Father, I've never seen a problem like this. I thought We included every problem on the cross when I paid the price for sin and took the curse. Somehow We left out their problem. How did We do that?" So then Jesus calls the Holy Spirit over, and the Holy Spirit says, "Oooooo! I've been moving over the whole earth, and I've never seen a problem like this problem. I don't know if We can come up with a solution for this one!"

Then you say, "Please, God, someway, somehow... please, God!" And God says, "I'm trying My best." God's pulling, Jesus is pulling, the Holy Spirit is pulling—they pull so hard on the problem that it throws a breaker in Heaven and the lights go out in the whole universe! So God says, "Gabriel, quit blowing that horn and come over here and help Us!" So Gabriel gets behind and starts pulling and you are still saying, "Please God, please God!"

> ***Jesus paid too high a price for your freedom for you to be bound.***

That's absolutely ridiculous! Yet, many times that is how we have prayed and approached God with situations and problems in our lives. What Jesus did, He did once through His blood and purchased eternal redemption for us.

Redemption simply means He purchased our freedom with His blood. Freedom from what? Freedom from sin, the dominion of Satan, and the curse of the law! Christ hath redeemed us from the curse of the law (Galatians 3:13). Praise the Lord, we are not under the curse anymore (Deuteronomy 28). We don't have to be sick, we don't have to be poor, we don't have to be depressed — we are no longer the victim!

Christ *hath* redeemed us from the curse of the law. It has already been taken care of — the transaction has already been made. Salvation is already in the account, and you can access it by faith!

> *...His own blood, having found and secured a complete redemption—an everlasting release for us.*
>
> ~ *Hebrews 9:12 (AMP)*

We have complete redemption. That means that God did not leave anything out—everything is already included. God thought about everything. He planned and provided freedom in every area. We have coverage in every area through faith in the blood of Jesus.

> *Faith in the blood—plus nothing, minus nothing—is all you need to enjoy God's best blessings.*

There are no *special problems* or *unique problems* that are not covered or that God has overlooked in the plan of redemption. Jesus paid it all! Jesus paid too high a price for your freedom for you to be bound. Jesus paid too high a price for your victory for you to be defeated. Let me shake you right now! Have confidence in the blood of Jesus! Declare your faith in the blood of Jesus. Get up now! You are released!

Application of the Blood

...When I see the blood, I will pass over you, and the plague shall not be upon you to destroy you...

~ *Exodus 12:13*

God's plan to bring the children of Israel out of Egypt required the application of blood. The blood was abundantly applied to the doorposts of their homes. The blood guaranteed their deliverance, protection, and freedom. The blood of Jesus must be applied today by faith. Faith requires having an understanding of the Word of God. Faith in His blood involves believing, speaking, and acting on His Word. We must understand the power in the blood of Jesus in our lives today. We must plead the blood of Jesus today and exercise faith in that blood. Faith in the blood—plus nothing, minus nothing—is all you need to enjoy God's best blessings.

By the Blood

We are redeemed by the blood. We have boldness by the blood. We are forgiven by the blood. We are righteous by the blood. We overcome by the blood (Revelation 12:11). We are blessed because of the blood. We are healed by the blood. The blood of Jesus carries all the facets of redemption throughout the Body of Christ. The blood of Jesus will never lose its power! Lift up your voice and mix faith with the blood of Jesus *now*!

Confession of Faith

- I know the truth, and it makes me free (John 8:32).

- The Gospel is the power of God to me because I believe it (Romans 1:16).

- I have been justified freely through the grace that is in Christ Jesus (Romans 3:24).

- Jesus obtained eternal redemption for me by His blood (Hebrews 9:12).

- I am redeemed by the blood of Jesus. I have been justified freely by His grace through the redemption that is in Christ Jesus and through faith in His blood. Jesus purchased my freedom with His own blood. I have faith in His blood because I understand the value and the power in it!

The storms of life come to all of us, but God has given us an anchor of hope that reaches into Heaven itself.

~ Mark Hankins

CHAPTER 20

Hope: Cheerful Expectation of Good

Trina and I visited the USS Midway in San Diego and were very impressed with this great aircraft carrier. This powerful ship is now retired and is visited by thousands of tourists each year. It was used as a defender of freedom during World War II, the Korean War, the Vietnam War, and the Gulf War. Having served for almost fifty years, it is still inspiring visitors. We were amazed at its capacity to carry over 4,000 men. As we stood on the flight deck, we saw that they could even launch or land two fighter jets at the same time. Its catapult system could launch a jet off its deck so fast that in less than three seconds it would be flying at 165 MPH. It was a fascinating tour.

The Anchor Room

I was as equally impressed with the "Anchor Room" as any other place on the ship. It is one of the larger rooms on the ship and holds the anchor that weighs 40,000 pounds. The chain that holds the anchor is wound around giant spools. Each chain link weighs over 130 pounds. The tour guide said that when the anchor went down to secure the ship, everyone on the ship could feel the vibration. The Anchor Room made me think about this scripture:

...Lay hold upon the hope set before us: which hope we have as an anchor of the soul, both sure and steadfast, and which entereth into that within the veil; Whither the forerunner is for us entered, even Jesus...

~ *Hebrews 6:18-20*

...Hold fast the hope appointed for us and set before [us]. [Now] we have this [hope] as a sure and steadfast anchor of the soul [it cannot slip and it cannot break down under whoever steps out upon it — a hope] that reaches farther and enters into [the very certainty of the Presence] within the veil, Where Jesus has entered in for us [in advance], a Forerunner having become a High Priest forever after the order (with the rank) of Melchizedek.

~ *Hebrews 6:18-20 (AMP)*

The anchor for your soul is this hope that reaches into Heaven itself. This anchor is both sure and steadfast. It holds fast in the very presence of God. When the strong winds blow, the anchor holds your soul steady. God says we must lay hold on this hope set before us. The storms of life come to all of us, but God has given us an anchor of hope that reaches into Heaven itself.

We belong to two worlds: The seen and the unseen. We have an inner, hidden life that brings us into touch with God, and an outer, bodily life by which we are in relationship with mankind.

~ *Andrew Murray*

God's definition of hope is different than the natural definition. Some think of hope as simply wishing, like someone throwing a coin into a wishing well for good luck. However, God's hope is much different. The Bible definition is "a cheerful, confident expectation of good." We have an anchor for our soul that gives us a constant, cheerful, confident expectation that God's goodness is ours. We can expect a miracle in every situation. What Satan means for evil, God turns for our good. This anchor holds us steady while miracles are coming.

Cheerful and Confident Expectation

...To make our approach unto Him in the most cheerful expectation of His blessing.

~ *Hebrews 10:22 (Doddridge)*

The Word says that Abraham "against hope...believed in hope." When it looked impossible, he believed it was possible. Hope is as supernatural as faith and love. These three abide forever: faith, hope, and love.

> *The storms of life come to all of us, but God has given us an anchor of hope that reaches into Heaven itself.*

Hope is eternal. This hope reaches beyond the seen into the unseen realm of God. We lay hold upon this hope. Because of Jesus, we live with a cheerful, confident expectation. This gives us tremendous inner strength that the world does not understand. We are happy and confident with a positive expectation in every situation in life. Christ in us is the "hope of glory." We expect the glory and goodness of God to win in life.

In Psalms 42 and 43, the psalmist David talked to himself saying, "Why are you discouraged...Hope thou in God...I will yet praise Him who is the health of my countenance." David repeatedly talked to himself and encouraged himself. The most important conversations you will ever have are with yourself.

Turn your expectations to God. One translation says, "expect God to act." I like that one. Hope holds you steady and changes your countenance. Look to the Lord Jesus and expect. Faith gives substance to our hope. Begin now to praise God and cheer up!

Rejoice in Hope

By whom also we have access by faith into this grace wherein we stand, and rejoice in hope of the glory of God.

~ Romans 5:2

Through Him also we have [our] access (entrance, introduction) by faith into this grace (state of God's favor) in which we [firmly and safely] stand. And let us rejoice and exult in our hope of experiencing and enjoying the glory of God.

~ Romans 5:2 (AMP)

We are able to "rejoice in hope" expecting, experiencing, and enjoying the glory and goodness of God. This hope will not leave us disappointed because the love of God is shed abroad in our hearts by the Holy Spirit (Romans 5:5). This is not a false hope or disillusion. This is certain through time and eternity. Notice faith, hope, and love working together. The anchor of hope holds your soul (mind, will, and emotions).

Now the God of hope fill you with all joy and peace in believing, that ye may abound in hope, through the power of the Holy Ghost.

~ **Romans 15:13**

The Amplified Bible says, "overflowing and bubbling over with hope." Something good is happening to you, in you, and through you! You are overflowing with a cheerful and confident expectation right now!

Confession of Faith

- I have a hope that is the anchor for my soul. Both sure and steadfast, it enters into the presence within the veil (Hebrews 6:18-19).

- The God of hope fills me with all joy and peace in believing. I abound in hope through the power of the Holy Ghost (Romans 15:13).

- I make my approach to God in the most cheerful expectation of His blessing (Hebrews 10:22).

- I have access by faith into this grace wherein I stand and rejoice in the hope of the glory of God (Romans 5:2).

- Hope makes not ashamed because the love of God is shed abroad in my heart by the Holy Ghost (Romans 5:5).

THE BLOOD
POWER TO DO
GOD'S WILL

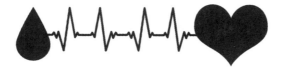

AND LET US CONSIDER ONE ANOTHER TO
PROVOKE UNTO LOVE AND TO GOOD WORKS.
~ HEBREWS 10:24

The blood flows through the human body from head to toe every twenty-three seconds providing oxygen and removing waste. In the same way, the blood of Jesus flows through the Body of Christ circulating continuously as we fellowship together. As the blood of Jesus flows there is a continuous supply of strength and a cleansing and removal of sin.

~ Mark Hankins

CHAPTER 21

Some Assembly Required

Now you (collectively) are Christ's body and (individually) you are members of it, each part severally and distinct [each with his own place and function].

> ~   1 Corinthians 12:27 (AMP)

Now here is what I am trying to say: All of you together are the one body of Christ and each one of you is a separate and necessary part of it.

> ~   1 Corinthians 12:27 (TLB)

But as it is, God has placed and arranged the limbs and organs in the body, each [particular one] of them, just as He wished and saw fit and with the best adaptation.

> ~   1 Corinthians 12:18 (AMP)

The Apostle Paul is the only writer in the Bible that describes the relationship of Christ and the Church as the relationship of a person's head and body. Christ is the head of the church and we are His body.

And hath put all things under his feet, and gave him to be the head over all things to the church, Which is his body, the fulness of him that filleth all in all.

~ Ephesians 1:22,23

When Jesus was raised from the dead, He was raised and seated *far above* and we were raised and seated with Him *far above*. Even if you are the little toe in the Body of Christ, you are still seated with Christ *far above* and the devil is under you. We have been raised, seated, and blessed with Him. That is the power of our identification with Christ.

Not only do we have a supernatural relationship with Christ, we also have a supernatural relationship with the rest of the Body of Christ. We must be properly related to certain parts of the Body of Christ for the impartation of life and power of Jesus to flow in us.

The book of Acts uses the word *assembled* many times. The place where they were *assembled* was shaken (Acts 4:31). Just like the tricycle box that you bought for your child said "some assembly required," there is some assembly required for the fullness of the glory of God in our lives.

We are instructed in Hebrew 10:25 to "forsake not the assembling of ourselves together." There is a greater anointing and authority when we get "assembled" in right relationships. There is a corporate anointing and corporate faith when we come together in Christ. Acts 4:23 says, "... they went to their own company." They had corporate prayer which brought corporate power and boldness!

Supernatural Relationship

That which we have seen and heard declare we unto you, that ye also may have fellowship with us: and truly our fellowship is with the Father; and with his Son Jesus Christ.

~ *1 John 1:3*

God has strategically placed supernatural relationships in each of our lives in the Body of Christ. The purpose of these relationships is to supply all of the vital ingredients that are necessary for our success. We must recognize and honor these relationships properly if we expect to get the fullness of the glory of Jesus and to do all the will of God.

There are members of the Body of Christ that carry revelation knowledge that we need in order to do the will of God. Supernatural relationships are important because there is a supply of revelation and of the Holy Spirit that is made available to us. It will come from those over us in the Lord, those around us in the Lord, and those under us in the Lord.

> *There is a corporate anointing and corporate faith when we come together in Christ. In the book of Acts they had corporate prayer which brought corporate power and blessing.*

One day the Lord told me, "There are important things you need to know that I will not tell you if I told it to someone you are supposed to be in relationship with. You will have to get it from them." God has revealed some things to others that are necessary for our success that we will only get when we recognize and receive from them as a significant part of the Body of Christ.

We must walk in love and recognize the importance of others in the Body. Different parts of the Body supply different, yet very necessary, ingredients for our success in doing the will of God. We cannot do the will of God by ourselves. We need each other!

Circulation of the Blood

But if we walk in the light, as he is in the light, we have fellowship one with another, and the blood of Jesus Christ his Son cleanseth us from all sin.

~   *1 John 1:7*

But if we [really] are living and walking in the Light, as He [Himself] is in the Light, we have [true, unbroken] fellowship with one another, and the blood of Jesus Christ His Son cleanses (removes) us from all sin and guilt [keeps us cleansed from sin in all its forms and manifestations].

~   *1 John 1:7 (AMP)*

When you were young, did you ever take a rubber band and tie it around your finger? What would happen? Your finger would begin to swell because of poor circulation. If the blood circulation was cut off long enough, you could actually lose your finger!

Have you ever seen anyone with circulation problems? The first thing they begin to lose is the function of their feet. The blood carries nutrients and oxygen. If the problem continues, it begins to affect the toes and the legs as well.

The Blood Gets Rid of the Trash

All of us collect trash at our house and are probably very thankful for the garbage man who comes every week. It is easy to gather lots of trash in one week!

The same is true spiritually. You may go to church on Sunday, but by the time you come back to church the next Sunday, you have gathered a lot of trash. Where do you get your trash from? There is trash coming from MTV, CNN, radio, the Internet, rap music, rock-n-roll music, and country music. You can really collect some trash! It's coming from momma, the in-laws, your work, kin folks, your husband or wife, and even your kids! If you skip church, you can collect some serious trash in two weeks!

One purpose of the blood in the human body is to rid you of any contamination. Your blood circulates through your body in less than sixty seconds from your head to your feet bringing nutrients and carrying away contamination. If the blood is not circulating, the garbage is accumulating.

In 1 John 1:7, the word *cleanse* refers to a continual cleansing. In other words, it is an on-going thing. The devil likes to keep the blood from circulating in the Body of Christ because he wants to isolate you from fellowship. As we walk in the light as He is in the light and have fellowship with one another, the blood of Jesus continually cleanses us from all sin.

> *The devil likes to keep the blood from circulating in the Body of Christ because he wants to isolate you from fellowship.*

Your blood also has certain messenger functions. If it is not circulating, you might not be getting the message! You might say, "I'm too tired, I just don't want to go to church tonight." Do you know what the devil is trying to do? He's trying to keep you from receiving the supply of the Word of God. You need to say, "I am going to church. I am getting rid of some trash right now because the blood circulates by fellowship in the Body of Christ!"

The blood of Jesus carries everything we need: redemption, forgiveness, healing, and blessing. Everything is in the blood. The blood will also carry away guilt, shame, condemnation, fear, and torment. The blood will supply what you need and get rid of the trash!

We Are Known by Our Love

By this shall all men know that ye are my disciples, if ye have love one to another.

~ *John 13:35*

The only way you can get along with God is to get along with others. Talent is developed in solitude, but character is developed among people. In other words, someone might say, "The Lord and I get along real good. Me and Jesus, we are tight," but they obviously can't seem to get along with any one else in the church, at the house, or anywhere for that matter! Jesus didn't say "If you just love Me, you are my disciples." He said that if you love *one another*, you are His disciples.

This reminds me of the story of a man whose friends put Limburger cheese under his nose while he was sleeping. When he woke up, he said, "Man, it sure stinks in here." Then he walked into his kitchen and said, "Well it stinks in here, too!" Then he went into his living room and said, "It stinks in here, too!" So he went out on his front porch, hoping to get some fresh air. Taking a deep breath, he looked up at the sky and said, "Man, the whole world stinks!" So anytime it stinks everywhere you go, you are probably carrying the stink with you right underneath your own nose!

> *You can tell how you are getting along with God by how you are getting along with people in the Body of Christ.*
>
> *- B.B. Hankins*

The first evidence that you are fellowshipping with God is that you want to fellowship with others. God loves people. If you don't love people, then you really can't say you love God. The blood circulates through fellowship. When the Body of Christ is assembled, there is a supply of life that is available that will strengthen your faith.

> *If a man say, I love God, and hateth his brother, he is a liar: for he that loveth not his brother whom he hath seen, how can he love God whom he hath not seen?*
>
> ~ *1 John 4:20*

My Dad, B.B. Hankins, used to always say, "You can tell how you are getting along with God by how you are getting along with people in the Body of Christ." In other words, if you cannot seem to get along with others because you always see their faults, then you are really not getting along with God.

> *If you want what God wants for the same reason that He wants it, you are invincible.*
>
> *- F.F. Bosworth*

Yes, people have problems. When you fellowship with people, you will find out what their problems are. But the blood of Jesus cleanses us from sin and all of its forms and manifestations. Fellowship with the Body of Christ will allow the blood to circulate and flush out the trash!

Find Your Own Company

Acts 4:23 says, "...they went to their own company." You can't run with every dog that hunts, but you ought to be able to run with some dogs! In other words, you need to know where you fit. Where is your company? Where is your place? While you are willingly supplying something in your company of believers, God will supply your needs.

Surrender Your Will

F.F. Bosworth said, "If you want what God wants for the same reason that He wants it, you are invincible." The blood of Jesus carries the will of Jesus. Jesus went through the experience at Gethsemane where He said, "Father, I want what You want for the same reason you want it!" He offered perfect surrender to the will of God. Jesus said, "I lay My life down. Not My will but yours be done. I want what God wants, no matter what it costs Me, for the same reason He wants it!"

When you plead the blood of Jesus, it gives you the power to surrender your life to God. Through faith in the blood, you can apply the blood of Jesus to your "want" and your "will." You can say, "By the blood of Jesus I don't have to have my way. I want what God wants for my life."

As you make these adjustments in your heart, God will take care of you in grand style! Plead the blood of Jesus when your disposition starts getting into a mess, criticizing and judging others. Say, "I plead the blood over my mouth, my motives, and my attitude!"

As you humble yourself before the Lord, He will lift you up. He wants to use you in your family, in your city, in your nation, and your generation. Thank God for His blood!

Confession of Faith

- God placed me in His body where He wants me to be (1 Corinthians 12:18).

- Christ is the head of His body, the Church. We are filled with His fullness (Ephesians 1:22,23).

- In Christ, there is fellowship with others in His body and with God (1 John 1:3).

- When I walk in the light, I have fellowship with Him, and Jesus' blood cleanses me from all sin (1 John 1:7).

- I am known as a disciple of Jesus because I walk in His love (John 13:35).

- I love God whom I have not seen and my brothers and sisters in Christ whom I do see (1 John 4:20).

- I walk in love and recognize the importance of others in the Body of Christ. I recognize and honor the supernatural relationships that God has strategically placed in my life. I expect to get the fullness of the glory of Jesus and do all the will of God.

Believer, I urge you, let every thought about the blood awaken in you the glorious confession, 'By His own blood, the Lord Jesus has sanctified me. He has taken complete possession of me for God, and I belong entirely to God.

~ Andrew Murray

CHAPTER 22

A Vessel of Honor

But in a great house there are not only vessels of gold and of silver, but also of wood and of earth; and some to honor, and some to dishonor. If a man therefore purge himself from these, he shall be a vessel unto honor, sanctified, and meet for the master's use, and prepared unto every good work.

~ 2 Timothy 2:20,21

We have probably all been to a museum and have seen things that were especially valuable because of who used them. A certain ink pen is special because Benjamin Franklin used it; a certain chair is valuable because Abraham Lincoln used it. You might see a gun that is valuable because it belonged to General Patton. You would probably see an automobile or airplane that is very valuable because a president or celebrity used it. In most cases, what looks like a very common thing, became very special because of who chose to use it.

Certain vessels become extremely valuable because of who they belonged to or who they were used by. The same is true spiritually. Because God chose us, now we belong to Him. It is the greatest honor to be used by the Master. He is the Potter and we are the clay. Though we have been damaged, He makes us again. He shapes us with His hands to be a vessel of honor.

God uses cracked pots to make vessels of honor (Jeremiah 18:1-4). In Acts 9:15, the Apostle Paul is called by the Lord, "a chosen vessel unto me." In Romans 9:23, we are referred to as vessels of mercy prepared to carry God's glory.

God's Honor Roll

Hebrews 11 is God's honor roll. There are some unusual and flawed vessels that God chose and used. Noah, Abraham, Sarah, Jacob, Moses, the harlot Rahab,

David, and Gideon are just a few of God's faith graduates. Today, He uses us according to His design and purpose. God uses unusual people as advertisement of His great mercy. God also wants to bless us so much that He can use us as advertisement of His goodness. Each one of us should volunteer for the program! He also uses us because we believe Him and we choose to set ourselves apart for His purpose.

> *By His own blood, the Lord Jesus has sanctified me. He has taken complete possession of me for God, and I belong entirely to God.*
>
> *- Andrew Murray*

Uncommon Vessels

When we understand the purpose of God, it is easier to enter the program. His plan is to make us vessels of honor to be used for His special occasions.

You certainly wouldn't want to go into surgery and hear the surgeon ask if anyone had seen his knife and the nurse say, "The last time I saw it was in the kitchen. We were using it to make a ham sandwich." No, you want that and every other instrument to be clean and used only for its special purpose.

The same is true with God. He wants us to be clean, holy, sanctified, prepared, and set apart for His special purpose. Abraham Lincoln said, "I will study, I will prepare, and my opportunity will come." The time will come when supernatural doors will swing wide open and you will be used by the Master.

A Set Time... A Set Person... A Set Occasion

The word *sanctified* means to make holy, to purify, to cleanse, to set apart, and to consecrate. It means to set apart something or someone for a special purpose. It is something that is taken out of its natural surroundings by God's command and is set aside or separated as His own possession and for His service — that thing or person is holy. Sanctified means not only separation from sin but also from what may be permissible. It is an act of God.

A sanctuary is not only a holy place, it is also a place of refuge and protection. It is a place of special blessing. It is something chosen by God. It is initiated at His command

and sanctified by His power. *Sanctified* can be a chosen place, a chosen time, a chosen thing, or a chosen person. A chosen vessel is something or someone set apart especially by God and for God.

> *For thou art an holy people unto the Lord thy God: the Lord thy God hath chosen thee to be a special people unto himself, above all people that are upon the face of the earth. The Lord did not set his love upon you, nor choose you, because ye were more in number than any people...But because the Lord loved you, and because he would keep the oath...Know therefore that the Lord thy God, he is God, the faithful God, which keepeth covenant and mercy with them that love him and keep his commandments to a thousand generations.*
>
> ~ *Deuteronomy 7:6-9*

God chose you, not because of your talent or brilliance, but just because He loved you. You are set apart for a set time and a set occasion. You have a designated and special purpose. You must run the race that is set before you. When you live by faith, everything is already set. The fight is set because God is on your side.

I like Psalm 105:19 in reference to Joseph: "Until the time that his word came: the word of the Lord tried him."

Joseph remained strong until his appointed time came and not only was he released from prison, but he also became a ruler in Egypt. There is a set time for the will of God and the plan of God.

The Unlimited Reach of the Blood of Jesus

As the will of God was worked out in Christ, we were the objects of His obedience. Jesus surrendered Himself spirit, soul, and body to the will of God. He sanctified Himself by the will of God for us. The blood of Jesus carries the power of His will. The choice Jesus made in the Garden of Gethsemane to do the will of God is in His blood for us.

The blood of Jesus cleanses every part of man. The blood of Jesus not only reaches into Heaven's holy place, it also reaches into the soul, the will, the conscience, and the heart of man. The blood cleanses the whole man.

By the which will we are sanctified through the offering of the body of Jesus Christ once for all.

~ *Hebrews 10:10*

And in accordance with this will [of God], we have been made holy (consecrated and sanctified) through the offering made once for all of the body of Jesus Christ (the Anointed One).

~ *Hebrews 10:10 (Amplified)*

There is no place the blood cannot reach. The blood of Jesus reaches into Heaven's holiest place and reaches into man's lowest place. It flows anywhere and everywhere sin or Satan has been able to reach or damage. Smith Wigglesworth said, "There's not one thing in me that the blood does not cleanse." The blood of Jesus reaches every part. Our will, purposes, motives, and ambitions are purged by the blood of Jesus. Through faith in the blood of Jesus, we are cleansed from sin in every form or manifestation.

> *There's not one thing in me that the blood does not cleanse.*
>
> *- Smith Wigglesworth*

When I was a teenager, my mother told me more than once, "You may get what you want, but you may not want what you get." That has happened to most of us more than once. When we want what God wants, we will never be disappointed. F.F. Bosworth said, "If you want what God wants for the same reason He wants it, you are invincible."

...The blood of Jesus Christ His Son cleanses (removes) us from all sin and guilt [keeps us cleansed from sin in all its forms and manifestations].

~ *1 John 1:7 (AMP)*

Sanctified by His Blood

How are we sanctified? Hebrews 13:12 says, "Wherefore Jesus also, that he might sanctify the people with his own blood, suffered without the gate." We are sanctified by His blood. The cleansing power of Jesus' blood sanctifies, cleanses, and sets us apart for God. It was offered once for all time, all people, all conditions, and all blessings! The blood of Jesus does the work! We overcome and are blessed by His blood!

We have boldness because of His blood. We are valuable because He chose us. He purchased us and cleansed us with His blood. He chose to use us.

I like what Andrew Murray said: "Believer, I urge you, let every thought about the blood awaken in you the glorious confession, 'By His own blood, the Lord Jesus has sanctified me. He has taken complete possession of me for God, and I belong entirely to God.'" We were very common until we were chosen and used by the King of kings.

...Through the blood of the everlasting covenant, Make you perfect in every good work to do his will, working in you that which is well-pleasing in his sight, through Jesus Christ; to whom be glory for ever and ever. Amen.

~   *Hebrews 13:20, 21*

For by one offering he hath perfected for ever them that are sanctified.

~   *Hebrews 10:14*

It was the perfect sacrifice by a perfect person to perfect some very imperfect people.

~   *Hebrews 10:14 (MSG)*

So with that one sacrifice He made us holy and brought us into perfect union with God.

~   *Hebrews 10:14 (Laubach)*

The words *sanctified* and *sanctification* are sometimes misunderstood as unreachable goals for Christians. The Apostle Paul actually addressed his letters to the "saints" at Ephesus and Corinth. These "saints" were some very imperfect people by Christian standards. Yet, Paul, by the Holy Spirit, called them saints or sanctified, holy people.

> ## *The blood of Jesus reaches into Heaven's holiest place and reaches into man's lowest place.*

Romans 5:20 says, "Where sin abounded, grace did much more abound." The blood of Jesus brings life, salvation, righteousness, healing, and blessing everywhere it is applied. How is it applied? "...Through faith in His blood" (Romans 3:25). The blood of Jesus is applied by faith. Romans 10:17 says, "So then faith comes by hearing and hearing, by the word of God." The Word of God teaches us what the blood of Jesus does for us and in us. When faith cometh—confidence cometh—joy cometh— and victory cometh!

Release Your Faith

For both he that sanctifieth and they who are sanctified are all of one: for which cause he is not ashamed to call them brethren.

~ Hebrews 2:11

Faith is released in words and action. We begin to act like Jesus did what the Word says He did for us. We continue to speak and agree with God with our mouth.

Our faith in His blood can actually grow and increase. Our understanding of the power of the blood of Jesus increases.

We were sanctified by God in Christ. Now God is our Father and we are in the family. Jesus calls us His brothers. We have the same access to the Father and the same blessing in Christ.

> *But of him are ye in Christ Jesus, who of God is made unto us wisdom, and righteousness, and sanctification, and redemption.*
>
> ~ *1 Corinthians 1:30*

> *According as He hath chosen us in Him before the foundation of the world, that we should be holy and without blame before him in love.*
>
> ~ *Ephesians 1:4*

> *Blessed is the man whom thou choosest, and causest to approach unto thee, that he may dwell in thy courts: we shall be satisfied with the goodness of thy house, even of thy holy temple.*
>
> ~ *Psalm 65:4*

God sees us in Christ and calls us redeemed, righteous, and sanctified. Our faith agrees with God. God has chosen us in Christ and enabled us to live "before Him" or "in His Presence" without blame. We have boldness to enter into the holiest place by the blood of Jesus.

A Royal Priesthood

1 Peter 2:9-10 says, "But you are a chosen generation, a royal priesthood, an holy nation, a peculiar people; that you should show forth the praises of Him who called you out of darkness into his marvelous light....which had not obtained mercy, but now have obtained mercy." God did not say, "Try to be..." or "Some day you will be..." He said, "You are!" It is important to agree with God and say, "I am who God says I am." When we identify with Christ, we see ourselves in Him.

In this verse, God says that we are chosen, we are royal, we are priests, and we are holy. As a priest, we have a right to enter the presence of God. As a priest, we also have a responsibility to offer spiritual sacrifices. As a priest, we have the power to procure blessing on others. Because of the new covenant, God calls believers a royal priesthood!

God has not only cleansed, separated, chosen, and blessed us, but He also wants us filled with His glory. He says in Exodus 29:43, "...the tabernacle shall be sanctified by my glory." Every hindrance has been removed so God can dwell in us. We now carry His glory. We are chosen vessels to live in His presence and carry His glory. We cannot produce any of this. Jesus produced it for us and does the work in us. However, we will not be forced to participate. We still have a choice.

See the Invisible… Choose the Imperishable… Do the Impossible

By faith Moses, when he was come to years, refused to be called the son of Pharaoh's daughter; Choosing rather to suffer afflictions with the people of God, than to enjoy the pleasures of sin for a season; Esteeming the reproach of Christ greater riches than the treasures in Egypt: for he had respect unto the recompense of the reward. By faith he forsook Egypt, not fearing the wrath of the king: for he endured, as seeing him who is invisible. Through faith he kept the Passover, and the sprinkling of blood, lest he that destroyed the firstborn

*should touch them. By faith they passed through the
Red Sea as by dry land: which the Egyptians assaying
to do were drowned.*

~ *Hebrews 11:24-29*

You can clearly see Moses made his choice by faith. By faith he chose...by faith he forsook Egypt...by faith he could see Him who was invisible...and by faith he applied the blood. Moses was a man of faith. He was a chosen vessel of honor. One time I heard Oral Roberts say, "If you can see the invisible, you can choose the imperishable, and you can do the impossible."

*If you can see the invisible, you can choose the
imperishable, and you can do the impossible.*

- Oral Roberts

We must surrender ourselves to the will of God to be a vessel of honor. We have a choice of what kind of vessel we will be. If we want to be chosen by God for special occasions, we must participate in the sanctification process. God starts and finishes it but not without our will.

We are sanctified and set apart for God's purpose and plan. We are not only separated from sin but also things that may be permissible. We are sanctified spirit, soul, and body (1 Thessalonians 5:23). I like to read on to verse 24, "Faithful is he that called you who also will do it." God is faithful and is working in you both to will and to do of His good pleasure!

Sometimes we suffer and feel alone in the separation process. I guess it would not have been so bad to be separate if you were in the harlot Rahab's house when the walls of Jericho fell down. Her house was separate, protected, and still standing by a scarlet thread hanging out of the window (Joshua 6). The red thread of the blood of Jesus sanctifies us. We are chosen by God to be used by Him through faith in His blood.

You Are God's Advertisement

...Ye shall inherit their land, and I will give it unto you to possess it, a land that floweth with milk and honey: I am the Lord your God, which have separated you from other people...And ye shall be holy unto me....

~ Leviticus 20:24,26

God wants His children to be blessed and to be a blessing. When people see the favor of God in your life they will say, "They must be a child of God." You are set apart by His presence and separated to possess the promises. You are separated to be blessed, not isolated. God wants to bless you and use you as advertisement of how well He treats His children. God will use your life as advertisement of His great love and mercy. God takes flawed and cracked people and reshapes them to carry His goodness.

> ## *Never underestimate the love and mercy of God.*

Never underestimate the love and mercy of God. It reaches your life and family in every area. The blood of Jesus sanctifies us to enjoy God's best blessings!

> *But of him are ye in Christ Jesus, who of God is made unto us wisdom, and righteousness, and sanctification, and redemption.*
>
> ~ *1 Corinthians 1:30*

God wants to use you as a priest to make intercession and as a king to take authority. He wants to use you to release blessing into the lives of those around you. Through the power of the blood of Jesus you can rise to be a vessel of honor.

Confession of Faith

- I purge myself to be a vessel of honor, sanctified and meet for the Master's use, prepared unto every good work (2 Timothy 2:20,21).

- I am sanctified by the offering of the body of Jesus Christ once and for all (Hebrews 10:14).

- Jesus calls Himself my brother (Hebrews 2:11).

- I am chosen in Christ to be holy and without blame before Him in love (Ephesians 1:4).

- I am God's dwelling place, and He sanctifies me by His glory (Exodus 29:43).

- God is faithful and will sanctify me spirit, soul, and body (1 Thessalonians 5:23,24).

- I am God's advertisement of His great love and mercy. The love and mercy of God are reaching my life and family in every area.

- I am a chosen generation, a royal priesthood, a peculiar people; that I should show forth the praises of Him who has called me out of darkness into His marvelous light.

- God has made Jesus to be my wisdom, righteousness, sanctification and redemption (1 Corinthians 1:30).

What you are looking at determines whether you live or die, succeed or fail, win or lose! This is no time for spiritual "attention deficit disorder."

~ Mark Hankins

CHAPTER 23

What Are You Looking At?

In walking by faith, your eyes must be focused on the right thing because what you view determines failure or success. Regardless of your circumstances or feelings, set your eyes on the blood. As you consistently gaze on the power of the blood of Jesus, you will begin to live in the reality of your redemption.

Faith Is Instrument Rated

Walking by faith can be comparable to flying an airplane. A good pilot knows to trust his instruments, even if they are contrary to his senses. How would you feel if the pilot on your next flight announced on the intercom: "Today, folks, I'm not going to look at my instruments or listen to the air traffic controller. I'm going to fly by my feelings. I think I can land us at our destination." You would want to get off that flight immediately!

If a pilot does not have instruments, he can only fly for 90 seconds without visual reference. That means when he goes into fog or clouds, he becomes disoriented. He may feel like he's going the right direction when actually he is off course. To fly safely, the pilot needs to be instrument rated – he must focus on his instruments instead of what he feels or perceives naturally.

What the pilot keeps in front of his eyes determines the success of the flight. A good pilot trusts his instruments to give him the true status of altitude, position, airspeed, etc. If he flies by his senses, the whole plane could crash.

> *We are not to live by our senses, but we are to live by faith - looking into the Word of God and fixing our eyes on Jesus.*

The same principle holds true for Christians. Whatever we are looking at determines whether we live or die, succeed or fail, win or lose. We are not to live by our senses, but we are to live by faith – looking into the Word of God and fixing our eyes on Jesus. As believers, we are not trusting our feelings, but following the guidance of the Spirit of God.

You Can Believe When You Look

Numbers 21 tells the story of how Moses prayed for the people who, because of their sin, were bitten by poisonous snakes.

And the Lord said to Moses, Make a fiery serpent [of bronze] and set it on a pole; and everyone who is bitten, when he looks at it, shall live. And Moses made a serpent of bronze and put it on a pole, and if a serpent had bitten any man, when he looked to the serpent of bronze [attentively, expectantly, with a steady and absorbing gaze], he lived.

~ *Numbers 21:8,9 (AMP)*

Can you imagine how hard it must have been for the Israelites to focus and keep their gaze on that brazen serpent while surrounded by the poisonous vipers biting at them and others around them? But when the people looked and kept on looking, they were healed and lived. This was a picture of how Jesus became a curse for us on the cross. When Moses held up the serpent on the pole, it represented our sickness, curse, sin, guilt, and shame. As we look at the cross, we can see that we were crucified with Christ.

> *And as Moses lifted up the serpent in the wilderness, even so must the Son of man be lifted up: That whosoever believeth in him should not perish, but have eternal life. For God so loved the world, that he gave his only begotten Son, that whosoever believeth in him should not perish, but have everlasting life.*
>
> ~ *John 3:14-16*

In the above scripture, the words "to lift up" are significant in the Greek. I like what William Barclay said:

> *The verb 'to lift up' is hapsoun. The strange thing is that it is used of Jesus in two senses. It is used of His being lifted up upon the Cross; and it is used of His being lifted up into glory at the time of His ascension into Heaven. It is used of the Cross in John 8:28 and John 12:32. It is used of Jesus' ascension into glory in Acts 2:33, Acts 5:31, and Philippians 2:9. There was a double lifting up in Jesus' life – the lifting on the Cross and the lifting into glory. And the two are inextricably connected. The one could not happen without the other.*

Believing on what God did for us on the through the blood of His cross brings that "lifting power" to our individual lives. Jesus used the word "believe" when speaking about focusing on the cross. When we look at what Jesus did for us on through the blood of His cross with an attentive, expectant, steady, and absorbing gaze, He calls that believing. The power that is in His redemptive work and written Word is released into our hearts to give life, healing, and blessing. Believing means that you see with the eyes of your heart. By meditating on redemption, you can absorb the power in it. You can receive the promises and what the blood has done for you in the death, burial, and resurrection of Christ Jesus. Remember what you are looking at determines whether you live or die, succeed or fail, win or lose.

> *A steadfast gaze on Jesus will remove all doubt and fear. There is saving power when you look at Jesus!*

Jesus Will Save You When You Look

Remember the classic story about Jesus walking on the water and how Peter got out of the boat to walk to Him?

Matthew 14:30, 31 in the Amplified Bible says, "...when he perceived and felt the strong wind, he was frightened, and as he began to sink, he cried out, Lord, save me [from death]! Instantly Jesus reached out His hand and caught and held him, saying to him, O you of little faith, why did you doubt?" The Living Bible says that when he looked around at the high waves, he was terrified. Here again you can see the effect your vision and focus have on your faith. A steadfast gaze on Jesus will remove all doubt and fear. There is saving power when you look at Jesus!

There's Power to Change as You Look

When it seems like freedom from old attitudes and lifestyles is impossible, you need to set your focus on the Word of God. The Bible is compared to a mirror that you keep looking into until you change. This is the wisdom you need.

> *For if any man be a hearer of the word, and not a doer, he is like unto a man beholding his natural face in a glass: For he beholdeth himself, and goeth his way, and straightway forgetteth what manner of man he was. But whoso looketh into the perfect law of liberty, and*

continueth therein, he being not a forgetful hearer, but a
doer of the word, this man shall be blessed in his deed.

~   *James 1:23-25*

But we all, with open face beholding as in a glass the
glory of the Lord, are changed into the same image from
glory to glory, even as by the Spirit of the Lord.

~   *2 Corinthians 3:18*

A supernatural transformation takes place when you keep your gaze fixed upon the Word, find scriptures that paint a picture of the answer, and allow the Holy Spirit to reveal the face of Christ and stamp it into your heart. As you look at His Word, receive God's blessing and transformation!

Receive Your Healing When You Look

My son, attend to my words; incline thine ear unto
my sayings. Let them not depart from thine eyes; keep
them in the midst of thine heart. For they are life unto
those that find them, and health to all their flesh. Keep
thy heart with all diligence; for out of it are the issues
of life.

~   *Proverbs 4:20-23*

Seeing and hearing the Word of God opens the door for the power of that Word to come into you. The power of God will displace any sickness and replace it with health – spirit, soul, and body. Faith in God will grow automatically as you focus on the healing found in the Word, and you'll find yourself believing for the impossible.

> ***The Word of God is the best cure for any physical, emotional, or mental problem.***

Pastor Yonggi Cho, who pastors the largest Full Gospel church in the world, recently shared how he confessed out loud one thousand times, "By Jesus' stripes I am healed." He received his healing as he focused his attention on that scripture, and by speaking it, absorbed its power into his spirit, soul, and body.

The Word of God is the best cure for any physical, emotional, or mental problem. Speak the Word like you take medicine: with diligence and regularity. Miracles and healing will take place when you look!

There Is No Time for Attention Deficit Disorder

What is the Holy Spirit saying to the Church in these end times? What should we be doing when there are financial storms, vipers of fear, disease, and troubled times surrounding us? What are we looking at? This is no time for spiritual attention deficit disorder! Focus on these powerful words from the Apostle Paul:

While we look not at the things which are seen, but at the things which are not seen: for the things which are seen are temporal; but the things which are not seen are eternal.

~ *2 Corinthians 4:18*

You can see invisible things and eternal things. Hebrews 12:1,2 gives us instructions for finishing this race with joy: "Wherefore seeing we also are compassed about with so great a cloud of witnesses, let us lay aside every weight, and the sin which doth so easily beset us, and let us run with patience the race that is set before us. Looking unto Jesus the author and finisher of our faith; who for the joy that was set before him endured the cross, despising the shame, and is set down at the right hand of the throne of God."

First of all, you are not alone – you have a mighty host in Heaven cheering you on. Secondly, you are to remove every weight and sin hanging on you and keep running with your eyes on Jesus as your focal point. The Amplified Bible says, "Looking away from all that will distract to Jesus, Who is the Leader and Source of our faith…" Forget those things you left behind. They are only distractions to trip you up. Keep an attentive, expectant, steady, and absorbing gaze on Jesus, the Author and Finisher of your faith. There is certain victory when you look at Jesus!

> *Keep an attentive, expectant, steady, and absorbing gaze on Jesus, the Author and Finisher of your faith. There is certain victory when you look at Jesus!*

Let us believe the Word of God and see ourselves crucified with Christ. Then we can see the believer's identification with Christ, which is the greatest revelation in the New Testament. Believing is seeing yourself in Christ in His death and triumphant resurrection with the eyes of your heart. Let your faith take hold of this truth –

that if you were crucified with Christ, then you were also raised and lifted up with Him. From that perspective, your eyes behold His majesty and glory as you reach your destination and see Him face to face. Let us finish our course with joy!

Confession of Faith

- Jesus became a curse for me on the cross. He paid the price for my sin, sickness, guilt, and shame (John 3:14-16).

- With an attentive, steady, expectant, and absorbent gaze, I keep my eyes on Jesus (Numbers 21:8,9).

- I have been crucified, raised, and lifted up with Him. I choose to keep my heart centered on God's Word (2 Corinthians 4:18; Proverbs 4:20-23).

- As I look into the mirror of the Word of God, I am changed. Thank You, Jesus, for healing me and setting me free (James 1:23-25).

Life in the Blood

The type or picture of blood of Jesus began in the garden when God Himself first shed the blood of animals to clothe Adam and Eve's nakedness after they sinned and lost the divine glory they were meant to have. He gave the first prophecy concerning redemption of all mankind. Because the first Adam had failed to obey, he passed his death nature to the entire race. Genesis 3:15 states the intention of the Creator of the universe to bring a redeemer on the scene who would restore all things to His original plan.

I will put enmity between you and the woman, and between your offspring and her Offspring; He will

bruise and tread your head underfoot, and you will...
bruise His heel.

~ ***Genesis 3:15 AMP***

After thousands of years had passed, we saw the fulfillment of this prophecy in Jesus Christ, the Lamb of God. Born of a virgin and from the divine seed, He had no sin of His own and carried in His body the very blood of His Father. God provided Him with a body to live among us, to experience every joy and sorrow of humanity. Jesus was born in the lineage of David and is the Seed of Abraham.

In His life on earth, He ministered as a man anointed by the Holy Spirit. Through His obedience and sacrifice, Jesus Christ, the Son of God laid down his life on the cross. He poured out all His blood in order to redeem the world back from Satan's claim. With His blood, Jesus conquered darkness and broke the grip of the spirit of fear. He bought mankind back with the high price of His very blood. This will be the song of the redeemed as we gather around the throne to worship the Lamb slain from the foundation of the world.

Through simple faith in this Gospel story, anyone may receive the life that comes from the Last Adam who is Jesus. His blood cleanses and imparts the life from God. Simply believing in your heart and declaring your faith that God raised Him from the dead makes you a member of a new creation. Believing and receiving Christ brings you into a new family and imparts the bloodline of a champion!

Pray this prayer to make Jesus the Master of your life and to receive the new life that comes from the blood of Jesus:

I believe in my heart that Jesus died on the cross for me. I believe He shed His blood to be the payment for my sin. I believe He was raised from the dead and is alive now. I believe He is Lord of everything and is my Lord. I surrender my life to Him who loved me and gave Himself for me. Jesus, I belong to you. I am now a new creation and receive Your life in my heart. I believe I have passed from death to life! God, You are my Father and I am Your child. My past and old things are passed away and the Holy Spirit lives in me. I am free from sin and I am born again. Thank You, Father God. Thank

You, Jesus, for all You have done for me. Thank You, Holy Spirit, for living in me and being my guide as I follow Jesus all the rest of my life! Thank You for filling me with joy and the water from Heaven. Now I am satisfied. I am now in the bloodline of Jesus, my champion!

Anytime God wants to change someone's life, He always touches their mouth.

> ~ *Mark Hankins*

Confessions of Faith in the Blood of Jesus

Let us hold fast the profession of our faith without wavering; (for he is faithful that promised.)

~ *Hebrews 10:23*

So let us seize and hold fast and retain without wavering the hope we cherish and confess and our acknowledgement of it, for He who promised is reliable (sure) and faithful to His word.

~ *Hebrews 10:23 (AMP)*

> *Inasmuch then as we have a great High Priest Who has [already] ascended and passed through the heavens, Jesus the Son of God, let us hold fast our confession [of faith in Him].*
>
> ~ *Hebrews 4:14 (AMP)*

> *Wherefore, holy brethren, partakers of the heavenly calling, consider the Apostle and High Priest of our profession, Christ Jesus.*
>
> ~ *Hebrews 3:1*

The confession of your lips that has grown out of faith in your heart will absolutely defeat the adversary in every combat. If you will hold fast your confession of faith in His blood and allow the Word of God to strengthen your faith, you will overcome your adversary, the devil.

Keep your focus on getting the Word in your mouth and in your heart. All of the answers you need are in His Word. Fight the good fight of faith. Remember that mere interest or belief in the blood is not enough to win. You must apply the blood of Jesus by believing and speaking His Word.

For verily I say unto you, That whosoever shall say unto this mountain, Be thou removed, and be thou cast into the sea; and shall not doubt in his heart, but shall believe that those things which he saith shall come to pass; he shall have whatsoever he saith.

~   Mark 11:23

Daily Confessions

Listed below are some daily confessions you can speak over your life. It's important to say what God has accomplished for you in the plan of redemption. Declare with your mouth what Jesus has done through His blood and the power of His resurrection. God's Word spoken through your lips will win in every conflict!

By His own blood, the Lord Jesus has sanctified me. He has taken complete possession of me for God. I belong entirely to God.

~   *Andrew Murray*

God is on my side,
For the blood has been applied.
Every need shall be supplied,
And nothing shall be denied.
So I enter into rest,
And I know that I am blessed.
I have passed the test,
And I will get God's best.

~ Trina Hankins

The blood of Jesus purges me of every defilement of the enemy.

The blood of Jesus keeps and guards my mind day and night.

The blood of Jesus prevents deception and aborts every attempt of the enemy to deceive me.

The blood of Jesus is my divine covering and protection against all the fiery darts of the evil one.

Yea, the Blood of Jesus is alive! So full of life and grace, it perfects that which concerneth me, reconciling everything in me to the perfect will of God every day and in every way.

~ Grace Ryerson Roos

Confession Scriptures

The following scriptures will help build your faith in the blood of Jesus. Read these scriptures on a daily basis. Underline them in your Bible. Write them on post-it notes and stick them all around your home or office. Meditate on these verses and speak them over your life every day. As you continually feed your spirit on the Word, faith will rise up in your heart, and you will find yourself walking in victory.

She fears not for the snow for her family, for all her household are doubly clothed in scarlet.

~ *Proverbs 31:21 (AMP)*

For all have sinned, and come short of the glory of God; Being justified freely by his grace through the redemption that is in Christ Jesus: Whom God hath set forth to be a propitiation through faith in his blood, to declare his righteousness for the remission of sins that are past, through the forbearance of God; To declare I say, at this time his righteousness: that he might be just, and the justifier of him which believeth in Jesus.

~ *Romans 3:23-26*

Who shall separate us from the love of Christ? shall tribulation, or distress, or persecution, or famine, or nakedness, or peril, or sword? Nay, in all these things we are more than conquerors through him that loved us. For I am persuaded, that neither death, nor life, nor angels, nor principalities, nor powers, nor things present, nor things to come, Nor height, nor depth, nor any other creature, shall be able to separate us from the love of God, which is in Christ Jesus our Lord.

~ Romans 8:35, 37-39

For the kingdom of God is not meat and drink; but righteousness, and peace, and joy in the Holy Ghost.

~ Romans 14:17

And, having made peace through the blood of his cross, by him to reconcile all things unto himself; by him, I say, whether they be things in earth, or things in heaven. And you, that were sometime alienated and enemies in your mind by wicked works yet now hath he reconciled In the body of his flesh through death, to present you holy and unblameable and unreproveable in his sight.

~ Colossians 1:20-22

It was through what his Son did that God cleared a path for everything to come to him – all things in heaven and on earth – for Christ's death on the cross has made peace with God for all by his blood. This includes you who were once so far away from God. You were his enemies and hated him and were separated from him by your evil thoughts and actions, yet now he has done this through the death on the cross of his own human body, and now as a result Christ has brought you into the very presence of God, and you are standing there before him with nothing left against you – nothing left that he could even chide you for; the only condition is that you fully believe the Truth, standing in it steadfast and firm, strong in the Lord, convinced of the Good News that Jesus died for you, and never shifting from trusting him to save you. This is the wonderful news that came to each of you and is now spreading all over the world.

~   *Colossians 1:20-23 (TLB)*

Let us therefore come boldly unto the throne of grace, that we may obtain mercy, and find grace to help in time of need.

~   *Hebrews 4:16*

Neither by the blood of goats and calves, but by his own blood he entered in once into the holy place, having obtained eternal redemption for us. For if the blood of bulls and of goats, and the ashes of an heifer sprinkling the unclean, sanctifieth to the purifying of the flesh: How much more shall the blood of Christ, who through the eternal Spirit offered himself without spot to God, purge your conscience from dead works to serve the living God?

~ *Hebrews 9:12-14*

By the which will we are sanctified through the offering of the body of Jesus Christ once for all.

~ *Hebrews 10:10*

For by one offering he hath perfected for ever them that are sanctified.

~ *Hebrews 10:14*

Having therefore, brethren, boldness to enter into the holiest by the blood of Jesus, By a new and living way, which he hath consecrated for us, through the veil, that is to say, his flesh; And having an high priest over the house of God; Let us draw near with a true heart in full assurance of faith, having our hearts sprinkled from an evil conscience, and our bodies washed with pure water. Let us hold fast the profession of our faith without wavering; (for he is faithful that promised).

~ Hebrews 10:19-23

Through faith he kept the passover, and the sprinkling of blood, lest he that destroyed the firstborn should touch them.

~ Hebrews 11:28

But ye are come unto mount Sion, and unto the city of the living God, the heavenly Jerusalem, and to an innumerable company of angels, To the general assembly and church of the firstborn, which are written in heaven, and to God the Judge of all, and to the spirits of just men made perfect, And to Jesus the mediator of the new covenant, and to the blood of sprinkling, that speaketh better things than that of Abel.

~ Hebrews 12:22-24

Wherefore Jesus also, that he might sanctify the people with his own blood, suffered without the gate. Let us go forth therefore unto him without the camp, bearing his reproach.

~   *Hebrews 13:12-13*

Now the God of peace, that brought again from the dead our Lord Jesus, that great shepherd of the sheep, through the blood of the everlasting covenant, Make you perfect in every good work to do his will, working in you that which is well-pleasing in his sight, through Jesus Christ; to whom be glory for ever and ever. Amen.

~   *Hebrews 13:20-21*

Forasmuch as ye know that ye were not redeemed with corruptible things, as silver and gold, from your vain conversation received by tradition from your fathers; But with the precious blood of Christ, as of a lamb without blemish and without spot.

~   *1 Peter 1:18,19*

But if we walk in the light, as he is in the light, we have fellowship one with another, and the blood of Jesus Christ his Son cleanseth us from all sin.

~   *1 John 1:7*

If we confess our sins, he is faithful and just to forgive us our sins, and to cleanse us from all unrighteousness.

~   *1 John 1:9*

And from Jesus Christ, who is the faithful witness, and the first begotten of the dead, and the prince of the kings of the earth. Unto him that loved us, and washed us from our sins in his own blood, And hath made us kings and priests unto God and his Father; to him be glory and dominion for ever and ever. Amen.

~   *Revelation 1:5,6*

And they overcame him by the blood of the Lamb, and by the word of their testimony; and they loved not their lives unto the death.

~   *Revelation 12:11*

Notes

The spoken Word of God is the voice of the blood covenant. Sing songs, hymns, and spiritual songs about the blood. Praise God for the blood.

~ Mark Hankins

Songs on the Blood of Jesus

..Be filled with the Spirit. Speaking to yourselves in Psalm and hymns and spiritual songs, singing and making melody in your heart to the Lord.

~ Ephesians 5:18-19

For He says, I will declare Your [the Father's] name to My brethren; in the midst of the [worshipping] congregation I will sing hymns of praise to You.

~ Hebrews 2:12 (AMP)

Thou art my hiding place; thou shalt preserve me from trouble; thou shalt compass me about with songs of deliverance. Selah.

~ Psalm 32:7

Many of the old hymns carry the redemption doctrine of the blood of Jesus. These timeless melodies have been passed on from generation to generation. Most of these great hymns on the blood were written during the 1800's which preceded some of the greatest outpourings of the Holy Spirit of that era. Remember, the blood and the Holy Spirit work together. As we sing about the blood, we honor the blood of Jesus. When we honor the blood of Jesus, the Holy Spirit will work. The Holy Spirit goes where the blood flows. So we can expect a move of the Holy Spirit as we honor the blood.

> *When we honor the blood of Jesus, the Holy Spirit will work. The Holy Spirit goes where the blood flows. So we can expect a move of the Holy Spirit as we honor the blood.*

I grew up singing many of the songs included in this chapter. The blood is something we must never stop singing about. Even if you don't know the melody, you can speak the words of these hymns by faith. Lyrics such as, "This is all my hope and peace, This is all my righteousness, nothing but the blood of Jesus," are great confessions of faith in what His blood has done and will continue to do for you. Be encouraged as you lift your voice because there is great victory when you speak or sing these lyrics by faith. We rejoice because our faith is in the blood of Jesus Christ and it will never lose its power!

When I See Your Blood
Trina Hankins

When I see Your blood
I know how much You love me
When I apply Your blood
My blinded eyes can see

When I speak Your blood
There's not one thing in me
The blood cannot cleanse
My heart, my soul, my mind
I surrender to the power of Your blood

There's not one thing in me, one thing in me
One thing in me that the blood can't cleanse
There's not one thing in me, one thing in me
One thing in me that the blood can't cleanse

I'm on the Way
Trina Hankins

I'm on the way, I'm on the road
I believe and I say I'm on the road.
Step by step I possess and I have what I confess

I'm on the way, I'm on the road.

God is on my side, for the blood has been applied.
Every need shall be supplied, nothing shall be denied.

So I enter into rest, and I know that I am blessed.
I have passed the test, and I will get God's best.

Child Produced by Love
Trina Hankins

I am worthy, accepted,
Chosen, perfected
By the power in Your blood
I'm a child produced by love

I can boldly draw near you by the blood
For the price has been paid to give me access
You bring me to the presence of my Father
Where I cry Abba, Daddy God.

In Your presence, I can see Your face
I come very close to your throne of grace
You renew my strength with Your strong embrace
And with joy I can finish this race

In Your presence, there's an anchor for my soul
You are the God of all hope
Now I'm satisfied for You made me whole
So I surrender to You all the control

When He Sees Me, He Sees Me in Him
Cindy Black and Trina Hankins

God had a plan from the beginning of time.
A plan to resurrect His man and restore the glory,
The glory he once had.
He sent His love in the form of His own Son.
He became the perfect sacrifice,
He gave His very life to rescue all of man

Chorus
When He sees me, He sees me in Him.
He no longer sees a sinner, an outcast or a beggar
Or what I once had been.
But He sees me through the blood,
The cross and the resurrection.
He sees me raised up, seated next to Him in Heaven.
When He sees me, He sees me in Christ

Now in Him I live and in Him I have my being.
He's clothed me in His righteousness,
He's canceled every debt and set this prisoner free.
Now I can boldly come to throne room of His grace.
There's no more condemnation,
I'm a new creation, created in Him

I See a Crimson Stream
Garfield T. Haywood (20th Century)

Chorus
I see a crimson stream of blood,
It flows from Calvary,
Its waves which reach the throne of God,
Are sweeping over me.

On Cal'vry's hill of sorrow
Where sin's demands were paid,
And rays of hope for tomorrow
Across our path were laid.

Today no condemnation
Abides to turn away
My soul from His salvation,
He's in my heart to stay.

When gloom and sadness whisper,
"You've sinned — no use to pray,"
I look away to Jesus,
And He tells me to say:

And when we reach the portal
Where life forever reigns,
The ransomed hosts' grand final
Will be this glad refrain.

There Is Power in the Blood
Lewis E. Jones (1899)

Chorus

There is power, power, wonder working power
In the blood of the Lamb;
There is power, power, wonder working power
In the precious blood of the Lamb.

Would you be free from the burden of sin?
There's power in the blood, power in the blood;
Would you o'er evil a victory win?
There's wonderful power in the blood.

Would you be free from your passion and pride?
There's power in the blood, power in the blood;
Come for a cleansing to Calvary's tide;
There's wonderful power in the blood.

Would you be whiter, much whiter than snow?
There's power in the blood, power in the blood;
Sin stains are lost in its life giving flow.

There's wonderful power in the blood.

Would you do service for Jesus your King?
There's power in the blood, power in the blood;
Would you live daily His praises to sing?
There's wonderful power in the blood.

Glory to His Name

Elisha Albright Hoffman (1839-1929)

Chorus
Glory to His Name, glory to His Name:
There to my heart was the blood applied;
Glory to His Name!

Down at the cross where my Savior died,
Down where for cleansing from sin I cried,
There to my heart was the blood applied;
Glory to His Name!

I am so wondrously saved from sin,
Jesus so sweetly abides within;
There at the cross where He took me in;
Glory to His Name!

Oh, precious fountain that saves from sin,
I am so glad I have entered in;
There Jesus saves me and keeps me clean;
Glory to His Name!

Come to this fountain so rich and sweet,
Cast thy poor soul at the Savior's feet;
Plunge in today, and be made complete;
Glory to His Name!

There Is A Fountain Filled With Blood
William Cowper

There is a fountain filled with blood
Drawn from Emmanuel's veins
And sinners plunged beneath that flood
Lose all their guilty stains

The dying thief rejoiced to see
That fountain in His day
And there may I though sinful too
Wash all my sins away

Dear dying Lamb Thy precious blood
Shall never lose its power
Til all the ransomed church of God
Be saved to sin no more

And since by faith I saw the stream
Thy flowing wounds supply
Redeeming love has been my theme
And shall be til I die

The Cleansing Wave
Phoebe Palmer Knapp (1839-1908)

Chorus
The cleansing stream I see I see
I plunge and oh it cleanseth me
Oh praise the Lord it cleanseth me
It cleanseth me yes cleanseth me

Oh now I see the cleansing wave
The fountain deep and wide
Jesus my Lord mighty to save
Points to His wounded side

I rise to walk in heav'n's own light
Above the world and sin
With heart made pure and garments white
And Christ enthroned within

I see the new creation rise
I hear the speaking blood
It speaks polluted nature dies
Sinks 'neath the cleansing flood

Amazing grace 'tis heav'n below
To feel the blood applied
And Jesus only Jesus know
My Jesus crucified

Redeemed How I Love To Proclaim It
Fanny J. Crosby (1820-1915)

Chorus
Redeemed, Redeemed
Redeemed by the blood of the Lamb
Redeemed, Redeemed
His child and forever I am

Redeemed how I love to proclaim it
Redeemed by the blood of the Lamb
Redeemed thru His infinite mercy
His child and forever I am

Redeemed and so happy in Jesus
No language my rapture can tell
I know that the light of His presence
With me doth continually dwell

I think of my blessed Redeemer
I think of Him all the day long
I sing for I cannot be silent
His love is the theme of my song

I know I shall see in His beauty
The King in whose law I delight
Who lovingly guardeth my footsteps
And gives me songs in the night

Nothing but the Blood
Robert Lowry

Chorus 1
O precious is the flow
That makes me white as snow
No other fount I know
Nothing but the blood of Jesus

What can wash away my sin
Nothing but the blood of Jesus
What can make me whole again
Nothing but the blood of Jesus

For my pardon this I see
Nothing but the blood of Jesus
For my cleansing this my plea
Nothing but the blood of Jesus

Nothing can for sin atone
Nothing but the blood of Jesus
Naught of good that I have done
Nothing but the blood of Jesus

This is all my hope and peace
Nothing but the blood of Jesus
This is all my righteousness
Nothing but the blood of Jesus

Yes I Know
Anna W. Waterman (20th Century)

Chorus
And I know yes I know
Jesus' blood can make
The vilest sinner clean

Come ye sinners lost and hopeless
Jesus' blood can make you free
For He saved the worst among you
When He saved a wretch like me

To the faint He giveth power
Thro' the mountains makes a way
Findeth water in the desert
Turns the night to golden day

In temptation He is near thee
Hold the pow'rs of hell at bay
Guides you to the path of safety
Gives you grace for ev'ry day

He will keep thee while the ages
Roll thro'out eternity
Tho' earth hinders and hell rages
All must work for good to thee

The Solid Rock
Edward Mote and William B. Bradbury (19th Century)

Chorus
On Christ the solid rock I stand
All other ground is sinking sand
On Christ the solid rock I stand
All other ground is sinking sand
All other ground is sinking sand

My hope is built on nothing less
Than Jesus' blood and righteousness
I dare not trust the sweetest name
But wholly lean on Jesus' name

His oath His covenant
His blood sustain me
In the raging flood
When all around my soul gives way
He then is all my hope and stay

When Christ shall come with trumpet sound
Oh May I then in Him be found
Blessed in His righteousness alone
Faultless to stand before the throne

Under the Blood
Eliza Edmunds (1851-1920) and
William James Kirkpatrick (1839-1921)

Under the blood the precious blood
Under the cleansing healing flood
Keep me Savior from day to day
Under the precious blood

Lord keep my soul from day to day
Under the blood under the blood
Take doubt and fear and sin away
Under the precious blood

The sinner's refuge here alone
Under the blood under the blood
Here Jesus makes salvation known
Under the precious blood

Lord with Thyself my spirit fill
Under the blood under the blood
And work in me to do Thy will
Under the precious blood

Sweet peace abides within the heart
Under the blood under the blood
And gifts divine their joy impart
Under the precious blood

The Holy Spirit hour by hour
Under the blood under the blood
Exerts His sanctifying pow'r
Under the precious blood

I've Believed the True Report
Charles P. Jones (1900-1991)

Hallelujah hallelujah
I have passed the riven veil
Where the glories never fail
Hallelujah hallelujah
I am living in the presence of the King

I believe the true report
Hallelujah to the Lamb
I have passed the outer court
O glory be to God
I am all on Jesus' side
On the altar sanctified
To the world and sin I've died
Hallelujah to the Lamb

I'm a king and priest to God
Hallelujah to the Lamb
By the cleansing of the blood
O glory be to God
By the Spirit's power and light
I am living day and night
In the holiest place so bright
Hallelujah to the Lamb

I'm within the holiest place
Hallelujah to the Lamb
I have passed the inner veil
O glory be to God
I am sanctified to God
By the power of the blood
Now the Lord is my abode
Hallelujah to the Lamb

On the Basis of the Blood
David Ingles © 1991

On the basis of the blood,
On the basis of the blood
I'm more than a conqueror
I'm a son of His love
There are no impossibilities
Just because I'm in the family
Reigning through life
On the basis of the blood

Christ came as a high priest
Of good things to come
He carried His own blood
He entered in once
Into heaven's sanctuary
Secured our redemption
Gave of Himself an off'ring to God

It was accepted our seal of redemption
The blood of our Christ God's holy Son
He bought for us a standing
Of eternal sonship
With all its rights and privileges
On the ground of His blood

The tokens of vic'try
Are before the Father
Now we have the legal right
To use Jesus name
We're overcomers
Through our testimony
We now have all
That His blood guarantees

Braggin' On The Blood
Terry Mathews

When I say I'm healed, I am healed
When I say I'm filled, I am filled
Some folks wonder about me, They think that I'm a fool
Listen, let me tell you, I didn't learn this in school

B-L-O-O-D
The Blood is good enough for me
Hanging there on Calvary
Jesus was made sin you see
I'm bathed and cleansed by the crimson flood
I'm braggin' on the Blood

When I say I'm free, I am free, When I say victory, victory
Some folks are sayin', Who do I think I am?
I am nobody but by the Blood of the Lamb

The Blood is eternal, It took my sin away
The Blood is ever speaking, Of a brighter day
I'm going home to Heaven, To be with my Lord

I can't wait to get there, To receive my reward
When they say, "Why should I let you in?"

The devil is defeated , And that is for sure
I am completed, I am secure
The Blood has given everything to me

The Blood gives me access, Into the secret place
The Blood is the assurance, Of a covenant of Grace

The Blood Will Never Lose Its Power
Andrae Crouch © 1966

Chorus
It reaches to the highest mountain
It flows to the lowest valley
The blood that gives me strength
From day to day
It will never lose its pow'r

The blood that Jesus shed for me
'Way back on Calvary
The blood that gives me strength
From day to day
It will never lose its pow'r

It soothes my doubts and calms my fears
And it dries all my tears
The blood that gives me strength
From day to day
It will never lose its pow'r

Because of the Blood
Stan Pody © 2007

Because of the Blood
I can come boldly
Because of the Blood
I can enter in

It was a perfect sacrifice
Jesus so freely gave His life
Because of the Blood
I can enter in.

By the Blood of the Lamb
Stan Pody © 2000

Once there was a time when man
Could not just enter in
Once a year the high priest
Made a sacrifice for sin
At best these men of old could
Only worship from afar
But now through the blood of Jesus,
I can worship where You are

By the blood of the Lamb
In Your Presence I can stand
By the blood I now am clean
In Your presence I am seen
"A Righteous Man"
So by the blood I stand

Not by works of righteousness
That I had done
But it's by the precious blood
Of God's own son
That I can boldly go into the Holy Place
And receive the benefits of His mercy and grace
Two thousand years ago the blood and water flowed
The price was paid on Calvary,
My debt no longer owed.

Under the Blood
Ryan Barnett

There are so many times I'm walking down life's road
I don't know where to turn, I don't know where to go
But no matter where God takes me,
There is one thing I know
It's by the blood of Jesus Christ
To Him I'm even known

I'm under the blood, under the blood of the Lamb
I am forgiven from every sin
Every sickness and every pain
Is under the blood of the Lamb
I am blessed with all blessings and righteous in Christ
I am more than a conqueror by His sacrifice
I have freedom from anything Satan has planned
Under the blood, under the blood of the Lamb

Although there will be weapons formed by the enemy
I know it is the blood of Christ that truly protects me
No matter where I go I plead the blood before
So I have confidence to walk through every open door
Everywhere I turn I know Jesus will be
There is no one greater than the one who lives within me
And now that I'm in Christ, my eyes can finally see
That it's only by His blood I have real victory

And one day God's own Son went up to Calvary
He suffered, bled, and died to pay the price for me
Because of Jesus' blood it is now I can be seen
A new creation in Christ
I am freed, blessed, and redeemed

Purchasing and Contact Information

Mark Hankins Ministries
P.O. Box 12863
Alexandria, LA 71315

Phone: **318.767.2001**
Fax: **318.443.2948**

E-mail: **contact@markhankins.org**

Visit us on the web:
www.markhankins.org

Books by Mark Hankins

Spirit-Filled Scripture Study Guide - $35

This is a comprehensive study of scriptures in over 120 different translations covering many topics including redemption, faith, finances, and prayer.

The Power of Identification With Christ - $15

This book focuses on the reality of redemption and your new identity in Christ. As a new creature, you have everything you need inside of you to succeed in life!

The Spirit of Faith - $15

If you only knew what was on the other side of your mountain, you would move it! Having a spirit of faith is necessary to do the will of God and fulfill your destiny. The spirit of faith turns defeat into victory and dreams into reality.

Faith Opens the Door to the Supernautal - $12.50

In this book, you will learn how believing and speaking opens the door to the supernatural in your life! God has given every believer a measure of overcoming faith.

11:23 – The Language of Faith - $10

Never underestimate the power of one voice! This book contains over 100 inspirational, mountain-moving quotes to "stir up" the spirit of faith in you.

Taking Your Place in Christ - $12.50

Many Christians talk about what they are trying to be and what they are going to be. This book is about who you are *now* as a believer in Christ.

Revolutionary Revelation - $15.00

This book provides excellent insight on how the spirit of wisdom and revelation is mandatory for believers to access their call, inheritance, and authority in Christ.

Let the Good Times Roll - $12.50

This book focuses on the five keys to Heaven on earth: The Holy Spirit, glory, faith, joy, and redemption. The Holy Spirit is a genius. If you will listen to Him, He will make you look smart!

The Secret Power of Joy - $12.50

This book shows believers how to bring the heavenly atmosphere of joy into the reality of their daily lives. This triumphant joy brings victory in every circumstance.

www.markhankins.org

Mark and Trina Hankins travel nationally and internationally preaching the Word of God with the power of the Holy Spirit. Their message centers on the spirit of faith, who the believer is in Christ, and the work of the Holy Spirit.

After over 40 years of pastoral and traveling ministry, Mark and Trina are now ministering full-time in campmeetings, leadership conferences, and church services around the world and across the United States. Their son, Aaron and his wife Errin Cody, are now the pastors of Christian Worship Center in Alexandria, Lousiana. Their daughter, Alicia Moran and her husband Caleb, pastor Metro Life Church in Lafayette, Louisiana. Mark and Trina also have eight grandchildren.

Mark is also the author of several books. For more information on Mark Hankins Ministries, please log on to our website, www.markhankins.org.

Acknowledgements

Special Thanks To:

My wife, Trina

My son, Aaron, and his wife Errin Cody
> Their children, Avery Jane, Macy Claire, and Jude Aaron

My daughter, Alicia, and her husband Caleb
> Their children, Jaiden Mark, Gavin Luke, Landon James, Dylan Paul, and Hadley Marie

My parents, Pastor B.B. and Velma Hankins, who are now in Heaven with the Lord

My wife's parents, Rev. William and Ginger Behrman

Recommended Reading List by Mark and Trina Hankins

1. *The Power of the Blood of Christ* by Andrew Murray
2. *The Blood* by Grace Ryerson Roos
3. *Christ the Healer* by F.F. Bosworth
4. *Ever Increasing Faith* by Smith Wigglesworth
5. *The Holy Temple of Jerusalem* by Chaim Richman

www.markhankins.org

References

Amplified Bible. Zondervan Publishing House, Grand Rapids, Michigan, 1972.

Barclay, William. *The New Testament A New Translation.* Collins, London, England, 1968.

Barclay, William. *New Testament Words,* The Westminster Press, Philadelphia, Pennsylvania, 1974.

Bosworth, F.F. *Christ The Healer.* Fleming H. Revel, Grand Rapids, Michigan, 1973.

Carpenter, S.C. *A Paraphrase of Ephesians.* A.R. Mowbray & Co. Limited, London, England, 1956.

Carpenter, S.C. *Selections from Romans and The Letter to the Philippians.* Spirit to Spirit Publications, 1981.

Doddridge, P. *The Family Expositor: or a Paraphrase and Version of The New Testament.* C & J Rivington, London, England, 1828.

Farstad, Arthur. *The Holy Bible: The New King James Version.* Thomas Nelson, Nashville, Tennessee, 1982.

Forbes, Matthew Miller and Duncan Greenberg, "The 400 Richest Americans," September 17, 2008.

Goodspeed, Edgar, J. *The New Testament, An American Translation.* University of Chicago, Chicago, Illinois, 1923.

Hudson, James T. *The Pauline Epistles, Their Meaning and Message.* James Clarke and Co., Ltd., London, England, 1958.

Jordan, Clarence. *The Cotton Patch Version of Paul's Epistle*. Association Press, New York, New York, 1968.

Kenyon, E.W. *In His Presence*. Kenyon Gospel Publishing Society, Inc, USA, 1997.

Laubach, Frank C. *The Inspired Letters in Clearest English*. Thomas Nelson and Sons, New York, New York, 1956.

Lovett, C.S. *Lovett's Lights on First John*. Personal Christianity, Baldwin Park, California, 1969.

Lovett, C.S. *Lovett's Lights on Galatians, Ephesians, Philippians, Colossians, 1 & 2 Thessalonians with Rephrased Text*. Personal Christianity, Baldwin Park, California, 1969.

Lovett, C.S. *Lovett's Lights on Hebrews*. Personal Christianity, Baldwin Park, California, 1983.

Lovett, C.S. *Lovett's Lights on Romans*. Personal Christianity, Baldwin Park, California, 1992.

Merriam-Webster.com, Bloodline.

Minirth, Frank, Paul Meier, and Stephen Arterburn. *The Complete Life Encyclopedia*. Thomas Nelson Publishers, Nashville, Tennessee, 1995.

Murray, Andrew. *The Power of the Blood of Christ*. Whitaker House, New Kensington, Pennsylvania, 1993.

Nelson, P.C. *Bible Doctrines*. Gospel Publishing House, Springfield, Missouri, 1971.

Peterson, Eugene. *The Message, The New Testament in Contemporary Language*. Colorado Springs, Colorado, 1993.

Richert, Ernest L. *Freedom Dynamics*. The Thinker, Big Bear Lake, California, 1977.

Richman, Chaim, *The Holy Temple of Jerusalem*, Carta, Jerusalem, 1997.

Roberts, Oral. *When You See the Invisible You Can Do the Impossible*. Destiny Image Publishers, Inc. Shippensburg, PA, 2002.

Roos, Grace Ryerson. *The Blood*. Carl Roos, Bartlesville, Oklahoma, 1984.

Songselect.com, Blood Songs.

Stewart, James, *A Man In Christ*. Hodder and Stoughton, 1964.

Taylor, Ken. *The Living Bible*. Tyndale House Publishers, Wheaton, Illinois, 1971.

The Distilled Bible / New Testament. Paul Benjamin Publishing Company, Stone Mountain, Georgia, 1980.

The Twentieth Century New Testament. The Fleming H. Revell Company, New York, New York, 1902.

Trumbull, Clay H. *The Blood Covenant*. Impact Christian Books, Inc, Kirkwood, Missouri, 1975.

Webster, Noah. The American Dictionary of the English Language, 1828. *www.cbtministries.org/resources/webster1828. htm*

Wigglesworth, Smith. *Ever Increasing Faith*. Gospel Publishing House,Springfield, Missouri, 1996.

Wikepedia.org, Human Blood, Bone Marrow.